Dedication

I dedicate this book to my husband, Bill, for his continuous patience, my son, Christopher, my friend, Linda Lyons-Bailey, for her invaluable time once more with last-minute editing advice, my other friends, and the various writing groups I am a member of.

I also dedicate this book to all those who have enjoyed the countless myths, legends, and the fantastical true stories from all over the world. For you are the ones who keep them alive and pass them on from generation to generation, around campfire and the hearth, on a ghost walk, and at your granny's knee. Without you and these stories, this book could not have been possible.

Acknowledgments

First, I'd like to thank my editor, Dinah Roseberry, for her wonderful guidance in both this book and my prior ghost book. I'd like to thank AVPA, for their dedication to saving historical sites, like Bacon's Castle and Jamestown Island. Thanks also to the various places and museums I visited and the people at these places who allowed me to interview them. I would like to thank L. B. Taylor for writing so many wonderful books of Virginian ghosts and to Hans Holzer for being the first author of the first ghost books I ever read, for they gave me many hours of enjoyment.

I would like to thank Brian A. Conley, Deborah Painter, and Terry Skylar of Ghost Fire Haunts for sending me some stories of the Tidewater region.

Contents

6 Contents

Foreword

Myths, legends, and fascinating true stories of Virginia...When one thinks of this subject, one probably has mental images of rural folk from a hundred years ago, telling already very old tales and stories to amuse themselves and their families after a long day working on the farm or in the foundry. But did you know that many myths and legends in Pamela K. Kinney's new book are only about twenty years old? One of these is the Bunnyman legend of Northern Virginia. Kinney has dug deep into old newspaper accounts to find out just why such a story came into existence, finding some surprising facts.

Another relatively new legend or myth concerns the restless Confederate soldiers who built a spectral fire at the end of Shirlydale Avenue in Henrico County. There was once a house used as a hospital there, but it was torn down in the 1980s and now the soldiers are out in the open, continuing what they had done for generations before the place was demolished.

Were sailors stationed in Norfolk, Virginia, during World War II, insulted by signs reading, "Dogs and Sailors Keep Off the Grass"?

Then there is the story of Three Sisters Bridge over the Potomac River, where three tall natural stones protrude above the waves, and where there is an alleged curse placed by three Native American women who drowned while trying to avenge the senseless murders of their lovers by another tribe. Since they could not cross the river, no one else was to cross it either. As late as 1972, the strange sudden storms that stir these waters collapsed the construction framework for the bridge. The Virginia Department of Transportation named it the Three Sisters Bridge when they finally succeeded in building it.

When you visit Virginia, as thousands upon thousands of tourists do annually, might you see more than historic Richmond and the Natural Bridge? Might you spy a Sasquatch, or even a Wampus cat? What's a Wampus Cat? Well, you won't know you saw one unless you read this book!

Pamela K. Kinney also relates some interesting myths about some of Virginia's most famous people. You'll find out not only what George Washington, Patrick Henry, and Edgar Allan Poe said, but what they DIDN'T say, which often becomes more famous and legendary!

What really happened between John Smith, Chief Powhatan, and the chief's young daughter, Pocahontas, back in the early 1600s? Hint: The Disney movie version is very far off the mark.

When the author visited some of the legendary haunted sites in the book first hand for research, she had some fascinating experiences of her own that left her wondering where legend ends and facts begin!

Try this book and you will definitely find it to be an amazing read.

~Deborah Painter
Author of "Hollywood's Top Dogs: The Dog Hero in Film."

Introduction

"Myths and legends die hard in America. We love them for the extra dimension they provide, the illusion of near-infinite possibility to erase the narrow confines of most men's reality. Weird heroes and mould-breaking champions exist as living proof to those who need it that the tyranny of 'the rat race' is not yet final."
~Hunter S. Thompson

Everyone participates in the reading of legends, myths, or folklore at some point in their lives. Who hasn't read Greek mythology in school, or the folklore of Paul Bunyan, or tall tales of famous, real people like Calamity Jane or Johnny Appleseed? And what about urban legends? Urban legends are myths told in modern society, in cities or online, unlike many of the old tales set in the countryside. Even now, these get passed around in emails or are posted on the Internet—stories about the serial killer with the knife hanging around Lover's Lane, Bloody Mary, the terrible smell under the bed in a hotel room or even the computer virus story that may have been true three years ago, but is still sent out as a warning.

A legend (Latin, legenda, "things to be read") is a narrative of human actions told about someone who existed in reality, once upon a time, but the true events have been twisted, making them more fascinating. Legend includes no happenings that are outside the realm of "possibility," defined by a highly flexible set of parameters. These may include miracles that are perceived as actually having happened. There is the specific tradition of indoctrination where the legend arose, and in which the tale may be transformed over time, in order to keep it fresh, vital, and realistic. It is kinda like that game you played with your classmates in school, where you whisper to the next person a story, and by the time it comes full circle, that story has changed drastically from what it began as.

A myth is a sacred or traditional story that concerns the origins of the world or how the world and the creatures in it came to be in their present form. Myths serves to unfold a part of the world view of a people, or explain a practice, belief, or natural phenomenon. Parables and allegories are myths. Nothing is supposed to be real about it at all, even if someone mentioned in the story is a real person, like some famous Virginians in this book. There are stories told about their habits or life that are not true.

Folklore is the traditional beliefs, myths, tales, and practices of a people, transmitted orally. It is popular, but unfounded beliefs. Or, as Merriam-Webster says: "traditional customs, tales, sayings, dances, or art forms preserved among a people."

The flavor of people and their culture, all interweaved with day-to-day life when settlers came to the New World. They brought with them their folk tales and beliefs, and founded new ones in the new country. Some old stories mutated into different ones. There were older tales told by the Native Americans who were already living in Virginia before the white man came. Then, when slaves were brought to the New World, they brought with them tales from Africa and changed them, molding them to fit their new home.

Today, in modern times, we continue this with urban legends. Who hasn't heard of the killer with the hook in lover's lane? Or what about saying "Bloody Mary" while staring into the mirror, hoping to make a ghost appear? There's the hitchhiking woman dressed in an evening gown who is picked up and climbs into the back seat, giving directions to an address to the driver. Once they arrive at the house, though, the driver discovers that she has mysteriously disappeared. When he goes to the door, he is told that his hitchhiker is the daughter of the owner of the house, and that she had been killed just after she left a party several years before, never making it home. But stories like the hitchhiking ghost existed long before they ended up as urban legends. I know I've read stories when it was a buggy or wagon being driven, not a car. So how many urban legends started as folk tales by those who colonized America?

Many of the legends and folk tales told by our ancestors have some kind of moral attached to them. These may be warnings. Watch your womenfolk and children, so that marauding Indians could not kidnap them. Don't dare approach some old woman living in the woods for a much-needed potion to rid one of an unwanted pregnancy, for she may conjure a spell and convince you to crawl into her oven to be cooked.

Virginia, like the other states in the U.S., has its own unique stories. The colonists who settled this Commonwealth were mostly common folk. They got up at the crack of dawn to farm the land or ply their trades and went to bed early to begin anew the next day. For entertainment, they did not have televisions or video games or the Internet. Instead, entertainment was tales told to their children, which had been told to them by their own parents, or to company at parties or around the campfire. Stories of the woman who lived alone in the cabin in the woods might be a witch who ate little children. Tales of giant hairy ape men seen and heard wandering the woods and mountains, or a tale of a howling thing in the middle of the road spread on purpose so that slaves would remain in their cabins at night.

Add tales from the Native Americans and those told by black slaves and you get a lot of wonderful stories to fill a book. When you sprinkle all that with countless sightings of Bigfoot, ghosts, monsters, and wild animals that aren't supposed to exist—even monsters from other states— you have a body of myth unique only to Virginia. Then there are those tales that sounds like fiction, but are real-life, bizarre stories.

No matter what anyone says, secretly, we all love reading these wondrous stories, for not only are they scary tales, or *incredible* tales, but a link to the Virginians of the past. These legends, myths, and even the strange true stories bring us closer together. Reading them, we stretch our fingertips across the centuries to hold hands with a colonist listening to a storyteller across the flickering flames of a campfire on a cold night. Whether based on a crumb of fact or not, these kinds of tales are a great way to pass the time. You can read them inside a warm house with a cup of tea within hand's reach during the middle of winter while a snowstorm roars outside, or on a vacation at the beach in the summer while basking in the sun.

So sit back in an easy chair, your cup of tea or coffee near at hand, and take a trip through the pages of history. Be prepared to learn about weird animals, vampires, werewolves, and other kinds of monsters that creep, even about ghosts that haunt cemeteries, houses, and other places. Take a page out of history and learn something new about famous Virginians, about the truths and untruths that have been told about them. Discover the tales that Native Americans and African-Americans of Virginia once told. And learn something about real people and animals whose own lives sounded like legends, but weren't.

It's time to learn the unique legends, myths and true tales that Virginia holds dear to its heart.

Chapter One
Ghostly Legends and Myths

In every state, in fact, in every country around the world, there are ghostly legends and folklore. Many are stories that are happening to people today, but there are many others that happened in the past and can not be authenticated. These are always told at sleep overs and at summer camp, at Halloween parties, and on ghost tours, too. With the Internet, many are posted in forums and on Web sites. Most of all, they always seemed to happen to a friend of a friend!

The Ghost Makes Him Behave—Portsmouth

There is a story told on the annual Ghost Walk in Old Towne Portsmouth each Halloween. Mike Hardy, an ex-Confederate soldier who always bragged about how many Yankees he killed in the Civil War, actually felt guilty for one death, a young drummer boy he shot in the back.

After the war, Hardy came back to Portsmouth and settled into a life of carousing and lechery. Later, though, as he passed by St. Paul's Church one night, he felt a strong compulsion to ask forgiveness for his sins. He entered the church and knelt. Just then, a voice behind him uttered, "I have long forgiven you for what you did to me."

Hardy whipped around and found himself face-to-face with the ghost of the drummer boy. The boy said, "Change your ways, Mike Hardy, or you won't be able to go where I am now." The ghost disappeared.

Chastened—or more likely scared—Mike Hardy changed his life around and became an upstanding citizen. It is said that when he was dying, he smiled and said he saw the Yankee drummer boy waiting to take him away.

Noisy Ghost-Varina

In the Varina Battlefield Cemetery, there is a cemetery on the right that has a very strange ghost lurking around the graves. He watches over the cemetery and the rumor goes that there's a water fountain in the yard. And if you drink from it, this spirit will make noises and sometimes throw things at you. He is believed to be a Confederate solder.

Haunted Theatre—Norfolk

Teddy Skylar of Ghost FIRE Haunts paranormal group (http://www. ghostfirehaunts.com/) told me that there's a legend about a theatre (the theatre does not want their name used) in Norfolk. In the very early days of the theatre, a stage hand named Ned tripped and fell from the rafters. He was accidentally hung and died. People claim to still see him back stage.

There is also a story in the same theatre about a small boy who fell from of the number 3 box seat, stage right. The child has been seen in the box, but only for a moment.

Lost in a Cave—Somewhere in Virginia

Along the New River, a local man found a cave and entered it in the mid 1900s. He became lost and did not get out for several days. Upon returning home, it was said that his hair had turned gray from his experience. He would never talk of what happened in the cave, except to say that no one would believe what he saw.

Haunted Statue and Mural at Virginia Military Institute-Lexington

On the campus of Virginia Military Institute in Lexington, there are written accounts that tears are seen falling down the bronze face of the Sir Moses Ezekiel's statue of "Virginia Mourning Her Dead." It is said that the statue may be mourning over the graves of the teen-aged VMI cadets who died in the Battle of New Market during the Civil War.

The statue isn't the only spooky VMI occurrence. A cadet—locked up by accident in Jackson Memorial Hall—claimed that not only did he see figures moving on a large mural of the same battle and flashes of gunfire, but he also heard sounds.

Worried Mother—Amherst

The story goes that a family bought an old farm and moved in. While the husband was out plowing and the wife had just completed her milking chores, the wife found a woman in black standing at the basement door, crying. Then the woman vanished. This happened for three days to the frightened farmer's wife. She told her husband and he told her that next time to ask what the woman wanted.

So when it happened to her again, she asked what was wrong. The ghost looked at her and said that in the field the farmer was plowing, her two children had been buried and she feared they would be dug up. The ghost told the woman that there was money she had hidden in the basement. She told her to take it and buy some tombstones for the two graves, that there would be plenty left over. The wife found the money as told. Then she and her husband discovered the two graves. They put a fence around the graves and marked them with special stones. Though the farmer and his wife never said how much had been found, afterwards they looked like a couple of considerable means.

Parted from True Love —Chatham Manor—Fredericksburg

Ever heard of the term, "looking for love in all the wrong places?" How about looking for love forever? The story goes that an English friend of William Fitzhugh, builder and owner of Chatham Manor, had sent his daughter to live there in an effort to break up her romance with a commoner. But her lover followed her to Virginia, planned an elopement with her, and gave her a rope ladder. He would wait for her in small boat in a nearby river while she used the ladder to escape. Unfortunately for her, George Washington learned of her plans from a maid and had his men arrest the suitor. The girl returned to England with her father and it is claimed that she later married. But she had vowed to return to Chatham Manor to find her lover. On June 21, 1790, when she died, someone said they spotted her ghost. It is said she returns every seven years on the anniversary of her death, still searching for her lost love.

Nasty Lady—Annandale

In Annandale, there are claims that the spirit of a lady holding a baby has been seen in Round Tree Park. They say she likes to torment the living who wander into the park at night. But she only appears when the fog rises.

Suicide Still Hanging Around in School Bathroom—Annandale

It is said that a boy who went to Annandale High School and committed suicide still haunts a boy's bathroom there, but not to sneak a spectral smoke. No, it is said he has been seen in the mirror in there.

My Lady Bridge—Middlesex

Once upon a time, one dark and stormy night, an unknown lady was driving her buggy home when the bridge flooded and she, the buggy, and the horse fell off it into the swirling waters below. The next morning they found her body. Now it is said that when you cross that bridge at night you can hear her banging underneath it.

Strange Ghostly Things in Honaker Hollow —Honaker

There is a tale that if you ride your horse out of the hollow in Honaker, someone—or something—will climb up behind you. And when you look back to see what it is, you'll find no one there!

There is also a certain old house in the hollow where people say that when they are inside, they have heard something on the roof. Whatever it is, it always tries to get inside by either coming through the windows or doors.

Spirit Pleased By the Play—Bridgewater

There is a college campus in Bridgewater that was supposed to have been built on Native American hunting grounds. But it isn't

Indians that haunt the place. No, it is haunted by the ghost of Mr. Cole. Reportedly, his spirit has been seen by members of the college drama club, musicians, and audience members. A story is told of what happens if he loves the performance of a play. At the end of one, lights will flicker rapidly, and a cold spot is felt near a particular seat on the balcony. It is also said that he can be seen sitting in that seat.

Of course, I couldn't find anything more about it and assume this is another tale that is more legend than an actual haunting.

Natural Bridge Hotel—Natural Bridge

When we pulled up into the parking lot of the hotel on August 28, 2008, it was a cloudy day and the hotel looked spooky, even threatening. My husband and I walked up the steps and indoors to the hotel reception, and there, we felt more welcomed. We received our room card key and information, learned where we could buy tickets to the Natural Bridge and the Caverns tour, then walked to our room, number 109, in the building next door.

Looking like many hotel/motel rooms we'd occupied, I found the bathroom to be older than the other hotels' rooms we had stayed in. Later, I found out from Margaret Miller, the Colonial Dining Room hostess, that the original hotel had a fire in 1963, burning the place and the gift shop across the street down to the ground. The one we now stayed in, plus the gift shop, had been rebuilt and reopened by August 1964. Unlike the earlier version, the dining room and the ballroom had been reversed, plus the wife of the then manager suggested a Flemish design, harking back to the Colonial days.

The hotel had been built, starting in the 1800s, and finished in three stages by the 1900s. In the 1960s, it had been owned by Mr. Claude Jessop, vice president of Pepsi Cola and founder of Trailways Bus, along with other stockholders. When he passed away, the other stockholders sold the Natural Bridge attractions and hotel to a group of real estate people out of Northern Virginia. This group still owns the attractions and hotel.

Now that the history of the hotel has been told, let's get on to the legend of the hauntings. Posted on several Web sites on the Internet, there had been a story passed around that the original owner of the hotel went insane and had killed his wife and kids one day. Apparently, it was the spirits of the wife and kids that wandered the grounds at night.

An aura of spookiness surrounds the Natural Bridge Hotel.

But that's a myth. I interviewed Amy Kasdan, the bartender working the Red Fox Lounge that night after dinner in the hotel's Colonial Dining Room. She had a lot of knowledge plus experiences with the hauntings. The main ghost that haunted the hotel is supposed to be Mr. Hunter, a manager of the hotel. He had committed suicide, either by hanging himself on a tree somewhere on the grounds or by shooting himself with a gun. Since both stories circulated, she could never find which way he really died—or, if hung, which tree, as the property is pretty large at 1100 to 1500 acres. His office was downstairs beneath the bar and that may be a reason he haunts the bar a lot, besides the office and rooms downstairs in the immediate area.

Another gentleman who worked for the hotel for fifty-one years and one month had also committed suicide—shooting himself with a 22 rifle. Speculation was that it was due to something he learned at a doctor's visit shortly before he did the deed, as he had always been a happy person and nice to everyone. The employees did learn that the doctor had prescribed him some antidepressants. He left a widow, who still lives in a small house nestled between the main portion of the hotel and the building our room was in. Though whether he also haunts the hotel, Amy wasn't sure.

Now the Red Fox Lounge used to be a standing bar, meaning only men were allowed in there to smoke cigars and drink. Of course, today, anyone over the age of twenty-one is allowed in there. No doubt, Mr. Hunter relaxed at the lounge many times.

One time, when Amy was working there and talking to another bartender, the door that led to the outside opened and closed, then however long it would take someone to cross the floor, the door to the bar swung open and shut. Amy called out, "Hey, Mr. Hunter, coming by today?" The funny thing about this, the first door can be explained by the wind pushing it open, but the bar door is harder to open and can not be explained.

Another time, the manager to the dining room felt heavy breathing on the back of her neck. A waitress from the Colonial Dining Room actually saw Mr. Hunter one day. She turned white as a ghost as he looked exactly like the photo they had hung up behind the front desk. (I haven't seen his picture, as it no longer is hung there.)

Once, when Amy had been working on the inventory late one night and had completed her duties, she signed out for the night. When she returned the next day at 6 pm she found all the bottles facing backwards. There was no way anyone could get in, as keys to the bar are never signed out except to the bartenders. Another time she came to find all the lights flickering and the bottles shaking. Amy also told me that Mr. Hunter is accused of being the one who likes to stop the hotel elevator on its way down.

One night, after she had went home, the maintenance men found the double doors to the dining room opened wide, so they went to shut them when suddenly they were shoved out the door and the door slammed shut on them!

Still another night, one of the front desk workers was talking with a maintenance man, after Amy left, when the front desk phone rang. The number showing indicated that it came from the Red Fox, which was impossible as she knew no one was there. The phone rang two more times that night, with the same number.

After I was done talking with Amy and taking photographs, Bill and I went to our room and went straight to bed at 9 pm, tired from all the walking we done. I woke up at 2:30 am. From where our stuff was, I could hear noises like someone picking up things and the loud rustling of paper. I turned on the light, but saw nothing. Shutting off the light, once again, noises filled the room. I switched the lamp on and got out of bed, heading over to where my electronic voice recorder was. I turned it on and told whoever was in the room that if they had something to say to tell it to the recorder. (Later, after I got home and uploaded the track onto my computer, there was a man talking really low during that time frame.)

Unnerved, I tried to go back to sleep and must have drifted off as I woke up again at 4:15 am. I was woken by whispering by my side of the bed. During all this time, my husband slept like the dead. I got up, used the bathroom, and crawled back into bed. I closed my eyes and tried to get back to sleep, but never did. Between 5:30 and 6 am, I felt cold air on my ear, as if someone kept blowing on it. I told it to let me sleep and got up and put on my voice recorder again. Again, I told the blower that if it had anything to say to me, to talk into the machine. I tried to get back to sleep after that but couldn't, so I decided to roll out of bed. It was 6:15 am and Bill still slept on.

I couldn't feel anything in the room with us, so I assumed whoever/whatever had been there had left. Next door to us was another room that I thought was unoccupied. When I heard from the other side of the bathroom wall the faucets of the sink coming on and then a short time later, the shower, I thought that I had been wrong and that someone had rented the room. But when Bill and I passed that room to get breakfast, the drapes were wide open and I saw the place was unoccupied, the beds made, and no sign of life.

Apparently our ghostly visitors had gone next door to get cleaned up after spending a portion of the night in our room.

Monster Museum—Natural Bridge

Mark Cline of the Lexington's Ghost Tours in Lexington also owns Professor Cline's Haunted Monster Museum and Dino Kingdom. His work has been seen in Alice Cooper's stage shows, Six Flags Theme Parks, and on NBC's Today Show. And his Haunted Monster Museum is one of the best "haunted houses" I have been in. That he uses a real Victorian house in Natural Bridge that looks perfect as a haunted house only adds to the heightened appreciation of being scared.

But what makes this even more interesting is the real ghost stories about the house. The building that held the original Monster Museum had caught fire and Mark Cline was lucky when he discovered this

More than automated ghosts haunt Professor Cline's Haunted Monster Museum.

house, which he bought for his attraction. Coined one of the seven weird wonders of the world by the *Washington Post*, the Monster Museum and Dino Kingdom was a mixture of the strange and wonderful.

I never got to meet Mr. Cline the day we were in Natural Bridge, but Bill and I were given a "tour" of the Haunted Museum and allowed to walk through the woods where dinosaurs tangled with Civil War soldiers.

While in the house, I admit to feeling uncomfortable about it, and maybe that was why the scary tour freaked me in some places more than normal. Later, when I talked to Amy Kasdan of Red Fox Lounge in the Natural Bridge Hotel, I learned that she and her husband had been in the place before Mark Cline had bought it. She had always been psychic and the place gave her the willies. She felt someone did not want her and her husband there. So she told him they had to get out.

A waitress at the Colonial Dining Room in the hotel told me the next day that there had been some ghost stories and legends circulating about the house. I didn't learn much, except that before Mr. Cline bought it for the Haunted Monster Museum, people say they heard weird sounds and saw *something* inside the place.

T-Rex taking on Civil War soldiers in Dino Land.

Next time you're in Natural Bridge, do the Haunted Monster Museum, but make sure that the hand you grab in the dark really belongs to your loved one. After all, the electronic ghosts aren't the only one haunting this place.

You can find out more about the Lexington Ghost Tours at http://www.lexingtonvirginia.com/attractionsb.asp?id=22 and about Professor Cline's Haunted Monster Museum and Dino Kingdom at http://www.naturalbridgeva.com/monster.html.

Screaming Woman of Natural Bridge Caverns —Natural Bridge

There is a story told about a screaming woman in Natural Bridge Caverns, the deepest caverns in Virginia. It seems that when they were digging into it to get the caverns ready for an attraction in the 1970s, a woman began screaming not far from them. The men thought someone was pulling a prank. It was dark, especially when their lanterns would

Where we bought our tickets for our tour of the Natural Bridge Caverns.

go out easily, becoming so black that you couldn't see your hand moving in front of your face. They contacted another group who went in there with them the next day, and of course, all heard the woman screaming again. The third time this happened, though, the woman screamed right in front of them. Frightened, they vacated the caverns and told the townspeople that they refused to work there. Of course, no body of a woman was ever found.

Now when my husband and I took the tour with a family on Thursday, August 28th, our guide, Matthew Hostetter, led us down into the bowels of the place, pointing out stalactites and stalagmites, Mirror Lake, along with parts of the rock forming into various animals and faces. When we got to the last stop, it was there he told us the legend of the screaming woman. He even turned off the lights to reveal how pitch black and scary it could be in there. Even *with* the lights, knowing bats soared high up in the ceiling, the caverns seem like another world, alien in nature. Still, it was magnificent.

Another take on the story of the screaming woman, which is more myth than truth, is one told by local school children in the area. During the Civil War, a woman took her young daughter into the caverns to escape the booming cannons and rifle fire from the battles happening in the area. Her daughter wandered away and she searched for the little girl but never found her. It is said that the little girl is the screaming woman—though a girl's scream is way different from a woman's. My husband's take on that story: It's the woman screaming as she searched for her child.

As we were heading back up to the surface, one of the photos I took did capture a small orb in the caverns. Is this the screaming woman's spirit? Hard to say.

Whatever the truth, it is easy to imagine anyone getting lost in the caverns and falling though a hole into another large room—even falling into the Lost River, breaking a leg, and drowning in the water. How many bleached bones of unwitting fools are in another part of the caverns? We may never know.

If you want to take the tour for yourself, you can find out more at the Natural Bridge Web site at http://www.naturalbridgeva.com/bridge.html.

Murdered at the Post Office—Crockett

There is a tale that a woman was at the Crockett Post Office late one night, checking her mail box. A murderer on the loose slipped inside while her back was to the entrance and, grabbing her, slit her throat. On the anniversary of her murder, a legend says that if you approach the building at night, you will hear her calling for help.

Did Not Listen to the Warning—Pigg River

There is a persistent legend of a man named Jesse Chandler. This man owned a piece of property about a hundred years ago, including a "dark hollow" off State Road 658 near the Pigg River south of Rocky Mount. One day, he went out to cut some firewood from an old oak tree. Someone called him back six times. He wanted that firewood bad enough to ignore the voice; so he tried for the seventh time, this time succeeding in cutting the tree. It fell and landed on him, killing him.

I caught a small orb on the wall of the Caverns as we ascended up to the surface at the end of our tour.

Devil's Slide Cave—Tazewell

In Tazewell, they say there's a cave that cavers frequent. It has strange phenomena connected to it. The legend claims that moans emulate from it, but no one can find out where they come from or the source.

The Thing in The Dip of the Road at Berkeley-Charles City

There's a legend about a ghost in a dip in the road that leads to Berkeley Plantation, home of two United States presidents and the first official Thanksgiving. The story goes that it is a young child who cries at night. It has been discounted by some to be only an owl. Others believed that plantation owners made up the tale to keep slaves in their quarters at night. After all, they felt the stories kept the slaves fresh for working in the morning and thought the ghost tale did more good than harm.

Creepy Bridge of Crafford Road—York County

There's a bridge on a section of road where Tour Road crosses over Crafford Road where, at night, weird things happen. The legend bandied about is that African-Americans were hung at the location. They say that an African-American woman in a white dress is seen standing on the bridge at the edge and then falls from it to dissipate just before hitting the pavement.

But the strangest stories that are told about this area are about vehicles that seem to stop running as they approach the bridge. Then, the same vehicles start up again when they are pushed past the "haunted" spot. Not all cars need to be pushed, though. Some say that their car shifts into neutral and will roll uphill some distance. Afterwards, they check out their cars and find handprints all over the paint.

Next time when you decide to drive down Crafford Road and approach the bridge, beware. For your car's engine may stop and someone may lend you a helping hand to push it—someone not of this world!

Murder at Tabb Residence Hall—Farmville

On the top floor of Tabb Residence Hall, there is another set of ascending stairs. Supposedly, these stairs lead to an abandoned abortion clinic that was the site of a murder. Allegedly, the murdered man still walks around the room.

A group of paranormal investigators have gone there and found the door locked, a handprint on it. The story about this bloody handprint is that it never can be wiped off. Some witnesses have seen or felt nothing, while others claim to have seen shadows and things moving out of the corner of their eyes.

What is the truth and what is myth? Maybe one day, somebody will find the ultimate proof.

Guardian of North Bend Plantation —Charles City

In L. B. Taylor's book, *The Ghosts of Williamsburg* II, I found references to a prized antique at North Bend Plantation in Charles City, Virginia. It is an oriental porcelain Foo Dog that dates to 1801. The dog is supposed to ward off evil spirits. But it seems that it isn't doing its duty. For North Bend is haunted.

Whatever the case may be about this dog, you can stay at the plantation, as it is a bed and breakfast and you will enjoy treating yourself to the history, besides to the hauntings. Built in 1801 by John Minge in historic Charles City County for his wife Sarah Harrison, North Bend Plantation became the home of the sister of William Henry Harrison, ninth president of the United States. The current owner, George F. Copland, is a descendant of the brother and sister.

As far as the ghost stories, it happened to one of the owners of the place, Mrs. Copeland. Awakened by something she heard in her bedroom, like pacing, she was worried because she was the only person there, and was concerned that it might be a burglar who had broken in. She made a call to her son, asking him to come. Then, when she heard the car outside, the mysterious footsteps ended. Both she and her son checked the house, but found no one. When he left, the footsteps started again. So she called him to come back and he stayed the night with her. All they could think of, was that it must have been General

Sheridan's spirit. Guests staying at the house have mentioned hearing similar noises at night, too.

Thirty thousand Federal troops camped in 1861 in the area of North Bend. This caused Thomas Wilcox, the owner at that time, to leave for Belle Air Plantation. He never returned. Union General Phillip Sheridan headquartered at North Bend while his troops built a pontoon bridge across the James River. The Web site pointed out that the desk used by the general is still at North Bend today.

North Bend Plantation is considered the best preserved of the academic Greek Revival Style buildings in Charles City County. Spacious at 6,000 square feet, it is a Virginia Historic Landmark and on the National Register. There are rare books, old dolls, along with spacious bed chambers with canopy beds, antiques, and private baths.

Next time you're in Charles City and want to stay at North Bend, don't bring any extra spirits with you. Just because the Foo Dog doesn't scare off the plantation's own haunts, doesn't mean it won't do its job on yours.

You can find out more about how to visit the plantation at their Web site at http://www.northbendplantation.com/.

Ghost of Murderer Haunting Governor's Mansion—Williamsburg

There is a myth about a ghost of a criminally insane escapee from Eastern State Mental Institution in the 1920s who slit a woman's throat. It is said that he haunts the wall in front of the mansion. Maybe after death he still is looking for other victims.

Williamsburg's First Serial Killer—Williamsburg

There is a myth that says the victims of Williamsburg's first serial killer still haunts the area of the mill where he stashed their bodies. Strangely enough, I could find nothing more about it, including the name of the mill, or even if it still exists today.

Help My Husband Please—Norfolk

A couple was murdered in the parking lot between Gresham and Main in Norfolk, Virginia, in November 2005. The killer or killers were never caught. There are tales that say the woman is still walking around bleeding from gun shot wounds, trying to find help for her dead husband. This usually happens for several nights towards the end of the November.

Story of the Farmer's Daughter —Haymarket Mill, Haymarket

There is a mill in the center of a gruesome legend. A farmer believed his daughter was responsible for giving her mother spoiled meat that killed her, so he decided to punish her. Most fathers would have turned her in to the local law enforcement, but this father did something different. He hung her from a meat hook on the fourth floor of the mill. Stories are told that her image could sometimes be seen on that hook until the place burned down some time ago.

Wildlife Preserve Also Place of Murder—Amelia

In Amelia, the Amelia Wildlife Management Area is a place for wildlife to live without being hunted. But it is also a place where there is a persistent myth told of murder, along with apparitions seen.

One of these apparitions is a charred lady. There have been two murders, with bodies discovered there. The dam nearby is the same one where a woman was seen dragging something. A body perhaps? I couldn't find anymore details though, so I think these are more legends then anything else.

The preserve is a protected area located in Amelia County near the town of Mason's Corner. Primarily upland habitat, it also preserves around 175 acres of bottomland hardwoods and beaver swampland along the Appomattox River. Much of the land was formerly used for farming; today it is managed to preserve wildlife habitat.

Searching for Her Children—Orange County, Near Gordonsville

The apparition of the Black Lady has been seen at Willow Grove Plantation. The place is on the National Register of Historical Places and is designated as a Virginia Historical Landmark. The legend goes on to say that she was a slave who worked in the house prior to the Civil War, her main duty to the owner's children. Attractive, light-skinned and tall, it is said that she also had two children by the owner. There is a rumor saying that he killed her and the two children and buried them somewhere on the property, although no gravestones have been discovered to prove this. Her spirit is still seen, no doubt searching for her murdered children. There are no stories of the children's spirits ever seen, just hers.

Murdered in the Church Belfry —Stafford County

There is a tale repeated online that a woman was murdered in the belfry of the Aquia Church in Stafford County. They say that her spirit has been seen from time to time peering from the window of the place. Is she still looking for the one who killed her?

Chapter Two
The Freaky Legends of Old House Woods—Mathews

For 200 years, legends have been passed down about this area near the Chesapeake Bay—Old House Woods, also known as Old Haunted Woods. It is fifty acres of pine woods and marshland near the tiny crossroads town of Diggs in Mathews County, northeast of Gloucester. The name, Old House Woods, took it from a large frame house, once known as the Fannie Knight house. It had a wood-covered plaster chimney and stood in the middle of the woods. Abandoned and falling into disrepair, it became known simply as "Old House."

It is said that pirates have been seen burying their gold on the property. A ghost ship is seen hovering over the woods. There's a legend told of British soldiers hiding Colonial treasure during the Revolutionary War here. They say skeletons in shining armor roam the woods as they wield their threatening swords. Ghost horses and cows appear and disappear before your eyes. There is even a story of a spirit that walks out of the water, dressed maybe in worn pirate clothing. Then, a Spanish Galleon rises out of the water with men leaping from it to the ground. Sounds of digging and the clanking of shovels fill the air. There are tales of two black headless dogs seen running through the woods.

All of these and more have been reported at different times of the year. There is even a rumor of a witch in a long nightgown who gives off a green light as she flies through the trees. Her long, fair hair streams behind her as her figure rises over the tops of the pine trees, and she wails loud, warning watermen and fishermen to take cover from a storm that suddenly whips up.

There are three reasons why these stories circulate about the woods. One concerns a legend that the crew of a pirate ship came ashore in the seventeenth century to bury their treasure of ill-gotten gains. The story goes on to say they perished in a storm at sea. To this day, it may be the spirits of those pirates who can be heard and seen searching for their treasure.

Another tale about the pirates had been written in the *Richmond Times-Dispatch* in 1973. The article said that Blackbeard himself intercepted the treasure, murdering the men. And that the men still haunt the woods, stopping anyone who dares to walk on the land.

Second possibility occurred in the second portion of the seventeenth century. Defeated at the Battle of Worcester in 1651, Charles II of England wanted to come to Virginia. To prepare for his trip, they sailed chests of money, plate, and jewels to the colony. The ship never reached Jamestown but sailed up the Chesapeake Bay and anchored off the mouth of White's Creek, near Old House Woods. The Royalists offloaded the treasure to be hidden, but a gang of renegade indentured servants attacked and murdered them. The murdering thieves only took a portion of the loot in their haste to escape. They planned to return later for the rest. But a sudden storm struck the area and their ship was capsized, all hands lost.

The last story supposedly happened in late 1781, before Cornwallis' troops were defeated at Yorktown. Two British officers and four soldiers had been entrusted with a large amount of money and treasure. These six slipped through enemy lines to head north. Not finding the British ship they had hoped to find, they buried the treasure in Old House Woods before they were found and killed by a unit of American cavalry.

No matter the stories of what makes the woods haunted, there have been those who have had experiences. Like Jesse Hudgins, who told what happened to him to the *Baltimore Sun* newspaper in the 1920s. The man ran a store in Mathews County back then. It seemed that he hitched his horse, Tom, to a buggy one October night when a neighbor with a very ill child came by, asking for him to get a doctor. He headed to town.

As he came upon Old House Woods, he spied, about fifty yards away, a light bobbing along the road in the same direction as he. His horse became frightened, but Hudgins got it to move forward as he wanted to find out what the light was. He had seen lights on the road at night before, but those were shining lanterns carried by men. This light seemed strange and unearthly, unlike those. When he caught up with the light, he saw a large man in armor, a gun over his shoulder with the muzzle like a fish horn. Not one sound did this stranger make and he seemed to be floating, not walking normally.

Scared, his horse stopped, not budging an inch more and Hudgins felt fear envelope him, too. The figure turned around to face him and just then, the woods came alive with lights and moving forms about a hundred yards away from him. Some of the others carried weapons like the figure in front of him, while others had shovels of the kind he never seen before and using them to dig beneath one dead pine tree.

Hudgins noticed then that the man in front of him actually was a skeleton! The armor seemed like glass and he could see every bone underneath it. Illuminated, the skull gave him a horrible grin. Raising a sword, it stalked Hudgins.

Hudgins lost it and fainted. His horse bolted, and the next morning his family found it cowering in the barn. They found him on the road, like he had fallen asleep. For months after, and until the day Jesse Hudgins died, he could never get that horse anywhere near the woods and the animal would always tremble and cower if he tried to force the issue.

Years later, there was an account in another newspaper about some young man whose vehicle had tire trouble one night near the woods. Kneeling on the road to get the old tire off, a voice behind him said, "Is this the King's highway? I've lost my ship." When the youth turned around and looked up, he saw with horror, a skeleton in armor. Screaming, he ran like a person pursued by demons and did not come back for the car until the next day.

The ghostly ship itself has brought some sightings. Like the time in 1926, when one fisherman, Ben Ferbee, in his boat had been fishing on a star-filled night. He noticed a full-rigged ship in the bay, and was puzzled by it as such ships were pretty scarce in those days. It began moving, heading his way with lights in every masthead and spar, and he grew scared. He thought they would run him down and he shouted at the sailors by the rails, but they ignored him. The ship passed by his boat, swamped by the water. Making no noise except for the most beautiful harp and organ music ever heard, it rose out of the water and up to the Bay Shore Road, the keel about twenty feet from the ground. He knew then it was a ghost ship! He pulled up anchor and aimed for home. As he left, he saw a ladder drop down from the ship and men with tools and other contraptions skittering down it to the ground. Not long after, he and his family moved from the cursed area.

Another sighting of the sailing ship is attributed to a fourteen-year-old boy from Mathews County. He and a buddy took a boat from the Mathews Yacht Club over to the Moon post office. Just after sunset, a mist shimmered over the water. A half mile from the mouth of Billups

Creek, they came upon the ship. It floated over the marsh and for another hundred yards, then dissipated.

Harry Forrest, a farmer-fisherman, also saw the ship. Before his death in the 1950s, Forrest saw armies of marching Redcoats, the "Storm Woman" and heard her wailings, and many times, his mother and he saw the lights in the woods. He had been fishing one day when right in broad daylight a full-rigged sailing ship came straight at him. He rowed to shore and watched as it lifted and sailed straight for Old House Woods. He also saw it another time, this time at night with his friends, Tom and Jack Diggs, as they passed through the woods.

Another story involved a farmer's wife who went to bring home their two work horses and drove them to the barn. At the gate, she called out to her husband to open it. He came out of the barn to tell her he had already put the horses in the stable two hours before. She turned to look at the horses and found two headless black dogs loping toward the Old House Woods. For years, there have numerous reports of headless cattle roaming the woods.

For centuries, stories and rumors of people and animal disappearances in the woods have been told. Like Lock Owens and Pidge Morgan a hundred and fifty-eight years before. Both had been driving their steer back from cattle auction, Lock's little black dog with them. They, and everything with them, vanished. Cattle would wander into the woods and never come back out again.

They say these animals would head for Old Cow Hole. One day, Old Cow Hole is filled with water, the next day it is dry as a bone. There are rumors of times when the woods have had a bad storm and a person has gotten soaking wet, then upon coming out of the woods, is perfectly dry. And there's Tom Pipkin who decided to search for the buried treasure in 1880. He took his boat on some channel—rumor said pirates had used it—going toward Old Cow Hole, never to be seen again. They found his boat, two gold coins of unknown age, and a battered silver cup, the items covered with mud. One coin bore a Roman head and letters "IVVS" on it. Feeling that it had been cursed, no one took Pipkin's boat and it was let to rot away on nearby Gwynn's Island.

Had the ghosts taken him, maybe drowned him, for daring to search for their buried loot? Whatever the truth is behind this story and all the weird tales, there is one warning repeated time and time again. People vanished into those woods, never to return.

If you get close to where the pirate treasure is hidden, you will never get out of those woods—ever!

Chapter Three
Ghostly Lights and Fireballs

In every state it seems there's the story of the brakeman who walks the tracks and is killed by a train, returning as a light bobbing along the tracks. But lights can be caused by other ghostly means. Like the phantom trains at Staunton and Otto River, and the ghostly ships at Lake Drummond and Rappahannock River. And of course, there are the fireballs, too.

Spook Light on Jackson Road—Suffolk

A "light" that has been sighted on Jackson Road in Suffolk in Nansemond County is the spook light. Sighted in late summer or early fall, people made calls about it back in 1951. Deputy Sheriff Hurley Jones was one officer who had investigated the sightings then and saw it himself. His description made it like a single automobile headlamp headed straight for the person who noticed it. Another policeman who saw it was Sergeant W. S. Damercon, saying it looked like the bright light of a train coming off the tracks.

Having been there myself, it's a stretch of road that starts out with a few houses, but most of the road is bushes on one side and woods on the other. Though it was daytime and my husband sat in the car next to me, that lonely section gave me an eerie feeling, especially as no cars roared down it while I took pictures. I could believe how anyone might imagine a ghostly light speeding down it at night.

Some people claim to have seen it all their lives. One resident of Jackson Road, Jeston Reid, acknowledged that his father had seen it seventy-five years earlier than the 1951 occurrence.

Jackson Road in Suffolk where a spook light has been seen.

Digging deep, it was found that the old Jackson and Whaleyville railroad ran along where now Jackson Road runs. Stories were remembered, that just like other incidents of lights seen along railroad tracks, that a flagman had been killed on the line in 1912. Many believed it is him who is the light. But others say that the "light" has been seen long before the flagman's death.

There are variations on the stories told of how he died. One has him as a member of the train crew that derailed in an accident. He lost his head when the cars piled on top of one another. Another tale has him struck down when he tried to warn the engineer about an oak tree that had fallen across the tracks, caused by a storm. The last legend mentions him trying to flag down a train in the fog as his child was seriously ill. The engineer failed to see him and the brakeman was decapitated.

Whatever the legend, it seems on Jackson Road, the brakeman is doomed to wander the tracks forever, searching for his head.

Ghostly Conductor of Cohoke Crossing —Near West Point

There is another such legend of a spectral light seen in West Point, Virginia. It seems that a conductor was walking along the tracks, lantern in hand, when a train passed by. A chain hanging off the train swung and decapitated him. There are stories of how he is seen walking the tracks, swinging the lantern back and forth as he searches for his head. Most times, it is just a bobbing white light you see. Sometimes it will follow you to Churchville Road and then will turn around to disappear.

For a hundred years, those who live in the Tidewater region have reported this light. It has been the thing to do for teenagers, to drive up to the site to wait for it to appear. Like my friend, Deborah Painter. She told me she even did it when she was younger. There are those who believe it is real. There are those who theorize it is swamp gas, or spirits from bottles of liquor some might have consumed before they arrived. It is, on dismal nights, mainly cloudy or rainy, that the ball of light has been seen.

At one point, in the sixties and seventies according to one King William County sheriff, W. W. Healey, it was like a circus, with so many people. He even had to say no to NBC's *Unsolved Mysteries* from filming there. Though it has died down since those days, he wouldn't go down there, more from fear of those who take guns with them to shoot at anything resembling a light.

There is a story of a lost train, that after the battle of Cold Harbor, a train in Richmond was loaded with wounded Confederate soldiers. It chugged its way to West Point, but never reached its destination. There have never been explanations as to what happened to it, but then, like a legend, no one likes to probe, but instead, enjoy the tale.

An interesting footnote to this legend is what did happen to Tom Gulbranson of Oceanview and his family in 1967. They had come there because Tom was an amateur psychic sleuth. He had visited the Cohoke site many times and on several occasions seen the light. The particular night in question was a freezing cold one. Nothing happened, but as he was packing up his camera equipment, the light appeared. Brighter then he had ever seen it before, the occupants from the car parked next to them flicked on their headlights. Startled, Tom saw the outline of a train in the light.

Light on the Tracks—Richmond

It is said that a light can be seen bobbing along the tracks at 102 Hull Street in Richmond. Even if you run to meet it, the light never gets any closer. It is thought to be a lantern of someone who has died there. There are also stories of fireballs and orbs seen at this spot.

Ghostly Light in Prospect Cemetery—Lebanon

There's a legend of a light that is seen in a Confederate soldier cemetery on North Church Street in Lebanon, right by Deer Spring's Trailer Court. Allegedly, if anyone travels to the cemetery after dark, they will be confronted by a floating blaze of fire. If they try to escape, it is said that the flame will follow, screaming in a very shrill voice. Some have said that it might possibly be a Civil War soldier carrying a lantern.

Someone admitted that when he was fourteen years old, he went to the cemetery one night. When he tripped over a tombstone, he spied an orange light and it shrieked at him. He bolted from the graveyard.

Author Richard Fulgham, met author L. B. Taylor for an interview at this cemetery one day. Nothing happened to them (during the daytime) when he took Mr. Taylor there. But later that night, he returned to the cemetery; he caught sight of reddish "lamps" moving around. The lights appeared to have emanated from quivering fog-like forms, translucent and glowing in the moonlight.

The caretaker of the cemetery says, "It's true there's Confederate soldiers buried there. People claim that on some nights, floating lanterns are seen. That the shrill voices heard might be 'Rebel yells,' blood-curdling to be sure."

Is an angry Confederate soldier still fighting the war? Or is it just another ghostly legend?

Lights in Cemetery—Lynwood

There is another graveyard near Lynnwood, Virginia, that lights have been seen. One person admitted to visiting the graveyard several times as a teenager, a few times late at night. He went on to say that the grave yard is fenced in and it is somewhat overgrown.

There are spots sunk in where the graves are and they only have plain rocks for headstones. But he never saw anything out of the ordinary here.

The story goes that the lights seen are supposed to be Civil War soldiers' lanterns.

Frightening Tales of Bethel Manor —Bethel Reservoir in York County

What was once a Revolutionary War and Civil War battlefield is now Bethel Reservoir. Between both wars there were many casualties that happened there. There are also legends that, before the Revolutionary War, it had been sacred ground to the Pamunkey Indians. There have been several drownings and also alleged kidnappings and rapes there. One of the most famous deaths by drowning happened in 1988 to Dewy Banks who fell out of a canoe. No one witnessed what happened, but his body was found several weeks later.

What has this to do with making the area a place to avoid, other than a place of bad karma? Strange occurrences have been reported there for years, including weird fog and balls of lightening. So the next time you want to go fishing there, watch out for sudden fog and lights.

Fireball of Bacon's Castle—Surrey

In 1675, a comet blazed across the night sky, ominous to the Virginia colonists. After that, scores of passenger pigeons flew in the sky and blocked out the sun. They did this for days. That spring, locusts swarmed, devouring trees of every leaf and all plants. The colonists became afraid, remembering when another comet lit the sky back in 1644. An Indian massacre happened not long after. So when Thomas Mathews's plantation overseer, Robert Hen, was found barely alive in a pool of blood, gasping out, "Doegs! Doegs!" before he died, no one was shocked that the events that followed transpired.

The Doegs were an Indian tribe known for attacks on white settlers. They made these attacks in retaliation for settlers killing some Indians caught stealing pigs and other livestock. This would lead to the large and violent Bacon's Rebellion, led by Nathanial Bacon.

Bacon's Castle.

Since Governor Berkeley didn't seem to be doing anything about what happened, the colonists turned to Bacon to lead a retaliatory attack against the Indians. He agreed and did, just after his own plantation had been attacked and his overseer killed. His forces pushed the Pamunkey Indians into Dragon's Swamp, then later killed 100 Susquehannocks and captured others.

Berkeley, angry at this, sent troops after Bacon and his men to capture them. It took a few weeks before Bacon surrendered and was brought before Berkeley. Forgiven when he repented, he escaped and returned with 600 men, capturing Jamestown. He demanded a repeal of harsh Colonial laws and to be given a commission to fight Indians. Berkeley granted both, but when Bacon was out chasing Indians, Berkeley sent troops after him. Bacon came back and sacked Jamestown, burning it to the ground.

Not long after that, Bacon became seriously ill (he had suffered an attack from malaria in Jamestown) and expired from dysentery October 26, 1676, in Gloucester, at the young age of twenty-nine. Soon after that, many of his followers were captured and executed by hanging. But before that, they had occupied a large brick mansion in

Surry. Known as "Allen's Brick House," it became known as "Bacon's Castle," ever since.

There's a small legend connected to Arthur Allen, that he may have been a Prince of the House of Hanover. The legend goes on to say that he loved the same woman that his twin loved. He had stabbed his twin, then escaped to the Colonies under an assumed name to start a new life, building his castle and raising his family.

There is one love story with Bacon's Castle that can not be proven and so may be a myth. A young woman in the 1800s met her lover, a farmer, in secret on a side of a cornfield. Her father didn't approve of him. But when one evening she had returned to Bacon's Castle, carrying a candle upstairs to her room, she tripped and her long hair caught fire from the candle flame. Not wanting her father to know she had been out, she kept quiet and ran from the house, back to the cornfield and her lover. She died in his arms, seriously burned.

Bacon's Castle is rife with hauntings, and there are those who say it is the work of the devil. Others believe it is the return of Bacon's men. Whatever they may be from, there are numerous sightings. From moaning in the attic to strange noises and unseen somethings passing by. The one of the fireball is interesting. Can this something be like the ball of light seen at Cohoke Crossing?

Seen as a pulsating, red ball of fire, it rises from the graveyard of Olde Lawne's Creek Church, south of the castle, and soars to the castle grounds, "floating or hovering" there before heading back to Olde Lawne's Creek Church graveyard to vanish.

Many sightings of this fireball have been reported over the years. What is it? Skeptics say it can be explained, while others call it a manifestation of the devil. One legend has a servant, a century or two ago, late doing his chores. Walking home in the dark, a red object appeared out of nowhere and burst, covering him in flames. He burned to death.

Another story talks about hidden money in the castle and that two men found it years ago while removing some bricks in the fireplace hearth in the second floor's west room. Since the money had been found, no one has seen the light since.

A third tale connects it with the spirit of Ginna Hankins, who had lived in the castle and went to the church to meet her sweetheart, Sidney Lanier, many times.

Another possibility: Why not the girl whose hair caught fire?

Whatever the story, when my husband and I took the tour of the place, we saw a house that stood the test of time. Out guide was very knowledgeable and we learned more then what the history books had ever reported.

But there are those who believe that the fireball is just a reminder of the comet that blazed across the night sky all those years ago. Whatever the truth or myth, the fireball and other stories that haunt the halls of Bacon's Castle are lost in the flames of time.

Chapter Four
Creepy Tales
of Great Dismal Swamp

A wonderful geological reserve that teems with animal and plant life is the Great Dismal Swamp. It lies on the Virginia-North Carolina line, bordering Suffolk and Chesapeake along its northern limits. With 120,000 acres, it measures forty miles long and fifteen miles wide, shrunk down from what it was in the 1600s. The heart of it is Lake Drummond, named for a Colonial governor of North Carolina.

Numerous legends have arisen here: like the ones of lovers cursed to haunt the swamp forever. The area is said to be inhabited by dragons, spirits, ghouls, and other strange beings. There are myths of Indian maidens abducted by strange "firebirds" and warriors battling to save them from these fiends. Eerie lights have been seen

The road that led to Lake Drummond—it was closed due to the wild fires they had.

dancing among the trees and scary sounds echoing at night bring heart-pounding terror. The local tribes in that area also say that the lake came to be due to the work of a phoenix-like being called the Fire Bird.

Is it only the imagination, or is it the truth? Whatever the case may be, Dismal Swamp is more than an ecological wonder; it's a fountain of myth and legend.

The Phantom Lovers of Dismal Swamp-Chesapeake

She fell ill just a few short weeks before their marriage. His betrothed was strong, beautiful, and healthy. Yet she faded away before his eyes. She gasped out her last breathe as the young man held her in his arms.

Inconsolable long after her body lay buried in the Dismal Swamp, he grieved for her, day after day and night after night. Scorning food and sleep, depriving himself until his mind broke under the strain, he became obsessed with the idea she was still alive. He figured her family had sent her away into the swamp and she just waited until he came to rescue her.

"I will find her," he said to his family, worried sick by his actions. "I will find her and hide her away from Death, so that he will never find her when he comes."

His family tried to convince him that she was dead, but he didn't listen. Instead, he escaped from them and plunged into the swamp. He wandered for days, living on berries and roots, and slept at night among the dark marshland.

One evening, he stumbled upon Drummond's Pond, a five-mile stretch of water in the middle of the Dismal Swamp. A firefly blinked on and off as it skittered over the black surface.

He yelled, "It's her! I see her light!"

He constructed a raft made of cypress branches he had gathered and used it to float out to join his lost love. But as he drew near the center of the pond, a wind sprang up and the raft tossed and tumbled in the sudden waves it caused. The man toppled from the raft and sank beneath the murky water, and drowned.

They say if you visit Drummond's Pond after the last light fades, just when the fireflies come out, you might see the phantoms of the man and his true love, united at last in death. Side by side, holding hands and carrying a firefly lantern, the lovers float across the pond on a raft made of cypress branches.

The White Deer and The Light

Black Jack the hermit took off in his boat one Christmas Eve, his only companion being his faithful hunting dog. He rowed across Drummond Lake, went down Washington Ditch and landed near White Marsh Road. Both man and dog left the boat to hunt deer for their dinner.

The Native Americans in the area claimed that white deer were protected by spirits. Jack's dog flushed out a white buck, the biggest deer Jack had ever seen. The buck froze, and when he fired at it, the bullet pierced its chest. But instead of falling, it bounded away. The dog gave chase, but lost it. Jack began to wonder if the local Indian stories were true then.

Later, the dog found a red buck and this one dropped easily when Jack's bullet hit it. He loaded the carcass in his boat and rowed for home. When it was almost dark, a blue-green light rose in the sky above the tree tops. Jack thought it was the moon rising, but then it zipped for his boat. It paused above his boat and illuminated the whole lake. Frightened, the hermit began to row faster.

When he got to his cabin, he dropped the buck and gave an order to his dog to guard the carcass, then went inside to gather the things needed to clean and dress it. He changed his clothes, sharpened his knives and went outside. Both his dog and the deer had vanished! Grabbing a lantern, he searched and found small patches of blood in the snow trailing back to the lake's edge. Stunned, he stood there, not knowing what to do.

Just then, a moan rent the air. Louder and louder it grew and sounding as if from the middle of the lake. He stared as the same blue-green light rose out of the water and over a giant cypress, covering the tree in its unnatural glow.

When the scream of a wildcat came, he jumped in his boat and raced downstream to the locks. He leaped onto shore and bolted to Captain Crockett's cottage. It was midnight when he banged on the front door. Black Jack streaked past Crockett when he opened the door. For three hours he sat in the cottage, not speaking, due to both being frozen and the fear he felt. Crockett gave him a mixture of honey, swamp water, and moonshine, and it freed him enough to blurt out his strange story.

The next morning Jack left, determined to find his dog and the missing deer. That night, Crockett dreamed of a white buck and the mysterious halo of light that surrounded its head. He awoke, knowing it to be a premonition of danger for Jack. So the next morning he traveled to the hermit's cabin and found the door wide open and the fire out. Jack was not inside. He searched outside and found Jack in a kneeling position in a thicket. The hermit had frozen to death. No other tracks surrounded him, and Crockett saw no signs of a struggle.

It is claimed that since then, on Christmas Eve between midnight and two in the morning, Jack can be heard gibbering about the light and the deer. At break of dawn, his dog and the missing red buck can be seen where he was found. Hunters fire at a white buck, but never hit it. The deer and the dog vanish into the underbrush.

The white deer that hunters shoot at and never hit could be the Indian maiden, Wa-Cheagles from the Indian myths chapter, except for their claim that it is a buck they saw and Wa-Cheagles became a white doe, protected by her warrior lover.

The Bride of Dismal Swamp

Once upon a time, a beautiful maiden lived at the edge of the swamp. She was to marry a lumberjack, and on the morning of their wedding, he set out to bag a deer for the feast at the wedding reception. He never returned in time for their wedding, so the bride, dressed in her wedding finery, searched for him. She too, never came back. Years passed and hunters would talk of seeing an apparition in the early morning on the south side of the lake. It was the bride, still in her bridal gown, baiting her hook as she sat on a log and cast out her line, most likely to catch a fish for her lover's breakfast. Then, like smoke drifting away, she vanishes.

Buried Treasure

A French vessel in the seventeenth century had blown off course and, to escape a British warship, hid in the Chesapeake Bay. The crew sailed up the Elizabeth River, where the ship ran aground. Taking as much of their plundered Dutch and Spanish gold coins as they could manage, the sailors abandoned ship and hurried into Dismal Swamp.

They buried their loot, but soon after, they were caught by British seamen and killed.

The story goes that, since then, people claim of hearing voices speaking in French, in the same area where, supposedly, the sailors had hidden their gold. Though over the years there have been gold coins found in this spot, no doubt the sailors are still trying to guard their treasure.

Chapter Five
Dancing with the Devil—
Charles City

There is a legend in Charles City County that so intrigued one children's author, Mary Quattlebaum, she wrote it into a children's book, *Sparks Fly High: Legend of Dancing Point*. It's a wonderful book with lovely pictures.

Dancing Point is a bit of land. The peculiar thing was that nothing would grow on this land bordering the James River. Nothing grew on it for centuries, while the land all around it was fertile and productive.

Even today, lights have been seen there. But for the story behind these ghostly lights, one must go back to a real man, Colonel Philip Lightfoot (1689-1748), ancestor of Harry Lightfoot Lee and Confederate General Robert E. Lee, for it was he who owned this parcel of cursed land.

They said that the Devil himself claimed that the land belonged to him and he caused its barrenness. He and Colonel Lightfoot fell into a dispute over the land. Like Daniel Webster, just not in court, and in his own way, Lightfoot agreed to a contest between the two of them, mortal and immortal, for this property. The contest would be in dancing, and the prize, the title to the land.

Both marched to Dancing Point at dusk, got rid of their coats and tricorn hats, built a large fire, and danced to the finish, around an old tree stump.

Dancing and dancing throughout the night. Lightfoot, as his name indicated, showed himself a highly accomplished hoofer. But the Devil didn't give up. He wanted to beat this mortal in competition. However, when the first rays of dawn stretched its fingers over the area, the Devil realized he'd lost. Limping away, humiliated, he traveled across the James River to Surry County, where old timers say he still lives.

Since that time, people see the flickering lights and when they venture closer, they claim they can see silhouettes of two figures dancing away furiously.

It seems that Colonel Philip Lightfoot can't rest quietly in his grave, but still must dance to beat the Devil.

Chapter Six
The Woman in Black—
Roanoke

Back in 1902, a "woman in black" held terrifying sway in Roanoke for several days. Dressed all in black, she wore a black turban on her head that she drew around her face and under her eyes, creating a black mask like a Moslem woman might wear. Completing the ensemble, she had a long, black cape covering her body. Though she never caused harm to anyone, her presence alone inspired fear. She would slip out of the shadows and melted back into them, leaving nothing of herself behind.

Her name was on everyone's lips and like the Boogey Man, she became the stuff of nightmares. No reason could be thought of why she caused such fear. Maybe the hysteria started just because she appeared in unexpected places and at hours that a woman shouldn't have roamed. Apparently, she only attacked married men, though even "attack" would be too strong a word to use. "Haunted" would seem more appropriate.

The first sighting happened to a prominent merchant. He admitted that he had been at his store late one evening, leaving after midnight. Out of the darkness, the woman in the black cloak appeared just behind him, his name a mere whisper from her lips. He began to walk faster and she did the same. Frightened, he bolted but she managed to keep up with him. What seemed odd, she appeared to be gliding and never exerted any real effort to keep up. After several blocks of silence, she spoke again.

"Where do you turn off?"

Heart beating wildly, he blurted, "Twelfth Avenue!"

He stumbled and the woman placed a hand on his shoulder. Her touch froze and burned at the same time. He tried to get away, but she held onto him firm.

"You're not the first married man I've seen to his home this night."

She let go, and the merchant bolted for his home. But she still had hold of him and he prayed that maybe he could get inside his house and slam the door on her fingers. Just as he opened the door and got partially inside, he realized that the cold pressure of her fingers had vanished. He hurried into the house and slammed shut and locked the door, taking no chances.

Two other married men, a telegraph operator and a hotel porter, also saw the apparition. She appeared to both late at night on the deserted streets of Roanoke. Approaching them in silence, she then called out to them by their names. Both men had been frightened and ran all the way home.

She remained in Roanoke for a few days, then disappeared, appearing next in the town of Bluefield. Another sighting also happened in March 1902 in Alma. Like Roanoke, this woman too appeared garbed in black.

Who was this mysterious woman in black who accosted married men? A scorned lover of one at some prior time? Or something else?

Just beware if you're a married man and out late one night on a deserted street, for the woman in black approaching you may not be someone you want a tryst with.

Chapter Seven
Keeping Lovers Apart—
Jamestown Island

There are those tales of lovers who, after their deaths, have flowers or trees sprouting from their graves, intertwining together and uniting the lovers' forever. But not in the case of James and Sarah Blair. This particular couple is buried in the cemetery behind Jamestown Memorial Church. There's a legend that a sycamore tree separates them in death— exactly what their families couldn't do in life.

In the 1700s, James Blair served as counsel to the British Government and later as governor of the Virginia colony. Historians regard him as the founder of the College of William and Mary in Williamsburg. He was considered to be handsome, too. One would think that this man would be considered a worthy suitor for any young woman. But not Sarah Harrison's parents.

Sarah Harrison was age seventeen. The oldest daughter of Colonel Benjamin Harrison of Wakefield Plantation, she was active in plantation social life and considered not only beautiful, but headstrong and full of life, too. She had many eligible suitors. One of the suitors, named William Roscoe, happened to be the one to whom her parents approved for her marriage.

Three weeks later after her engagement had been announced; she met James Blair and fell in love with him. This love affair was doomed from the start, not only because of her engagement to Mr. Roscoe, but because her parents did not like the fact that James was twice her age. In those days, any girl who married an older man became a disgrace to her parents, since society viewed such marriages as a sign of the girl's family's failing finances.

Jamestown Island Memorial Church.

Being headstrong though, Sarah did not stay away from James. Legend has it that her fiancé, William Roscoe, died of a broken heart after she broke their engagement. Not long after, she and James married. Her parents did not attend the wedding and would have nothing to do with the couple. They tried many things, from trying to have it annulled to even drawing up legal papers. During a trip to see an attorney about this, Colonel Harrison, his wife, and their youngest daughter were killed when lightning during a storm struck their carriage.

The Blairs went on to live happily as man and wife until Sarah passed away in 1713 at the age of forty-two. Never forgiven by her family, she could not gain entrance into the Harrison family plot and instead was buried in a stone crypt just outside it, in a small cemetery within grasping fingers reach of the Jamestown Memorial Church on Jamestown Island.

James and Sarah Harrison Blair's graves—no sycamore tree between them.

James lived another thirty years. When he finally died in 1743, he was laid to rest in another stone crypt about six inches from his wife's tomb.

In 1750, a sycamore tree began to grow next to James' crypt, right between his tomb and his wife's. Nothing was done to prevent its growth and it grew and grew until it shattered the bricks between the two crypts. This caused Sarah's headstone to move into the nearby Harrison plot, only a short distance from her parents' and her sister's graves.

The story doesn't end there. Not long ago, the old sycamore tree, grown very large, died and was cut down. The broken bricks and shattered tombs had been left as they were. Not long after, another sycamore tree sprouted in the very same spot. By all appearances, it appeared that the Harrisons still worked from beyond the veil to keep their daughter from James.

When my husband and I went to Jamestown Island one extremely windy and cold October 28th, we walked to the church and the fenced-in graveyard. There, we found both graves side-by-side. Actually it seemed that all the graves had been placed in rows of two, just behind the church itself. Had volunteers of the APVA finally dug out the sycamore tree sapling, roots and all, so nothing more would grow, or had James finally convinced his in-laws that he and Sarah belonged with each other, at least after death?

I like the romantic version better, don't you?

Chapter Eight
Black Dogs of Virginia

The Black Dog is a common occurrence in many hauntings. Most of the tales come from Great Britain. Stories such as this are surprisingly common and some of them notably ancient. Sightings of such creatures are in a class of their own in the ghost world. Ghostly black dogs have been seen throughout Britain with few counties being left unaffected, though the form and identity of the beast may differ.

Apparitions of this sort may be distinguished from normal flesh-and-blood black canines by features such as large or glowing eyes—sometimes only one—their ability to appear or disappear out of thin air or into and out of the ground, no head, two heads, or the ability to change their size or appearance.

The Black Dogs go under many names depending which county you are in. In the north of England in counties such as Yorkshire and Lancashire, you will hear names such as Guytrash, Shriker, or Barguest; in East Anglia and Norfolk, you will hear Black Shuck, Skeff, or Moddey Dhoo; and in the south of England, you will hear names like Yeth or Wish Hounds. The origin of the word *Guytrash* is unknown, but Shuck can be traced back to the Old English *Scucca*, meaning Demon, while Barguest may come from the German *Bargeist* meaning "spirit of the (funeral) bier." The demon association is sometimes emphasized by the title "Devil Dog." In the south, *Yeth* means *Heath*, while *Wish*, in a similar vein, is an old Sussex word for marsh. This name for the hounds is widely used in Sussex, but the origin also seems linked to the term Witch Hounds, which is also common. Whether there is any connection between the two is unknown. The names may only be referring to the fact that these dogs are often seen in wild country places. In many places, the dogs are seen as omens of death. To see one means either a portent of your own death or the death of a family member.

But you don't have to go to the British Isles to see one. There have been some of these beasts reported in Virginia. There's a legend of one that has been seen in Goochland, big as a young calf as it roamed the county. Sightings of it have always been reported to be near the State Farm, at the entrance to Thorncliff, and also at Chestnut Hill Bottom. Unlike Black Shuck in England, this one has never portended the death of anyone. There have been no tales of this animal seen since 1900 though.

Often, like the traditional Black Dogs seen in Britain, it would appear out of nowhere, trot alongside someone on foot or horseback or in a buggy. Even though it looked fearsome and was very big, it didn't harm anyone. Some, though, didn't want the dog accompanying them and would shoot at the animal. The bullets would just pass through its body, frightening the shooters, while the dog just kept trotting beside them.

A lawyer named P. A. L. Smith, Sr. used to walk from his house to the State Farm, where he caught a train into Richmond. On many evenings when he returned, he would find the black dog beside him as he headed home.

A woman who lived near the State Farm claimed that the dog entered her house by opening the screen door. She said that it walked over to her old-fashioned icebox, unfastened the door, took out some food, and then shut the door and left the house. An interesting side note about this woman's house was that other strange phenomena also happened there. Many would come to see the windows and doors of her house rock and rattle for no obvious cause, so when she told of the food-stealing Black Dog, many believed her.

Another Black Dog story is set in southwest Virginia, in the Saltville area. In the past, the roads became black and dusty, packed down with cinders from a factory there. Travelers on some of these roads swore they heard footsteps behind them, or saw dust clouds rising, but no horse or wagon would be visible. There would be reports of a dog, black as pitch, encountered on these roads too. It would keep pace with the frightened person and lope through ditches alongside the road, leap fences or pass through them, and go through water, no splashes seen. Some would say that the beast would jump up right behind them as they rode their horse down the road, spooking their horse and them.

A man named Tom Hurt reported an encounter with the Black Dog in the 1900s. When his shift ended at the Mathieson screening plant, he walked home. The dog appeared and followed him for a quarter of a mile. Tom decided to test it, so he threw several rocks at it, aiming for the white mark on its head. Instead of hitting the animal, the rocks apparently passed through and left it unharmed. Tom shot five lead balls from his gun into it, but once again, the dog was unhurt. Frightened, Tom felt he had to destroy it. But as they neared British Row, the dog bolted ahead and vanished at a large bridge on the road. Just then, Tom heard a woman's panicked voice, screaming. Worried that the dog could be attacking someone else, Tom got a neighbor from a nearby house to help him search for the woman. It didn't matter. Even with lanterns, they could find neither the woman nor the dog.

Though other residents of Saltville say they have seen it from time to time, its mystery remains unsolved.

In Mathews County, there is a legend of two black, headless dogs seen running in the woods of Old House Woods.

Then there's the spectral hound of Blue Ridge.

According to the tale, this massive black hound was seen along Skyline Drive during the late seventeenth century. At that time, there was a pass traveled by people going from Botetourt County to Bedford County and also used by visitors accessing the mineral springs. Just at sunset, along the wildest section of this pass, the black dog would appear. It would pace in a listening attitude for 200 feet and then return back the way it came. It did this each night, starting at sunset and dissipating at the crack of dawn. The animal's legend grew from one end of the commonwealth to the other. Some believed it was sent by some master to watch, others thought it was a witch dog. No matter what they thought, all were frightened by this apparition.

During one night with a full moon, a party decided to arm themselves and make it through the pass, dog or no dog. As they approached, they saw a dog bigger than any dog they had ever seen before. They urged their steeds on. But the horses snorted with fear, and in spite of whip, spur, and rein, would not go near the dog. The dog kept pacing as if no one was near. The men were unable to make the pass by horseback until daylight. Their comrades laughed at them when they told the tale.

So they decided to wait in ambush with guns, kill the animal, and bring in its hide. As the last light of day faded away, the dog appeared and began his march as usual. They fired at him, over and over. Not one bullet appeared to hit it. Frightened, the hunters fled back to civilization.

And so, the dog continued to do this each night for the next seven years, until one day, a beautiful woman came over from Europe, searching for her missing husband. Eight years before, he had come over to make her a home in the new land. She had traced him to Bedford County, but at that point, it was as if he'd vanished off the face of the earth. There seemed to be nothing more she could do, until she heard of the tale of the great black dog that night after night kept vigil on the pass. She begged to be taken there, wondering if it was her husband's dog. When the dog saw her, he came over to her. He laid his head in her lap, then stood up and walked a short way, pausing to look back as if making sure she followed him. He led her to a large rock and with a whine, began to dig at the ground. Suddenly, with a low wail, he vanished.

The woman told the others to dig at that spot, but at the time they had brought her there, no one thought to bring digging implements. Someone galloped off on horseback to get some. When he came back with the tools, they dug until they found the skeletons of a man and a dog. The man's bony hand had a seal ring circling one finger. He also had heraldic embroidery in silk that the woman recognized as something she had made for him. They removed the bones for proper burial and she returned home. According to the legend, after that day, the dog was never seen again.

Another spectral canine is a headless one that some say they have seen in the Northern Neck area of Virginia, east of Fredericksburg. It appears in creek bottoms when mists often rise above marshes. This headless beast is said to wander for the most part, in the lower section of the Neck—mostly alone, though there are occasions that he is joined by a companion. This companion is not always one shape, but three different ones— a white mule, a headless man, or another dog, this one sporting a head with glaring red eyes. Though not black as the other spectral dogs seen in Virginia, it is brown and large as a calf. It wears a chain around its neck that drags on the ground and rattles as it moves. The legend goes on to say that it is seen at night, between Cockrell's Neck and Heathsville, and only after or before a local resident's death.

There is a belief that the Devil pays visits to people in the form of a dog. Most of these visits are to men who lead notorious, wicked lives—like the story of an old rich man who owned a lot of slaves and led a wicked life. He had been married four or five times, each wife would become ill and die, or be found dead for no apparent reason. With their deaths, he inherited a lot of money. When his slaves died, he wouldn't let anyone come help bury them. It was thought he killed them.

As he lay dying, the neighbors came to sit with him. It was midnight and everyone expected him to die at any time. There came a noise at the door. Someone got up and opened it. A large black dog with eyes as big as saucers and glowing like balls of fire stood there. It entered and walked up to the bed. It reared up to place its front paws on mattress at the foot of the bed and stared at the old man. The old man screamed that the Devil had come for him. He tried to escape by getting out of bed, but fell back and died.

As for the dog, without a sound, it turned around and went back out the door, never to be seen again.

The last spectral dog spooky story is set on the Eastern Shore, in the Seymour House in Accomac. An elderly aunt was visiting the house and grew ill while there. A strange black dog no one knew or had seen before appeared mysteriously on the stairway. No reason had been given why, but one of the household shot at it on the fourth step as it began to climb the stairs. The animal dissipated, and when they searched, they couldn't find it. The aunt passed away four days later. Had this creature been about to steal her soul? Or was this a foretelling of her death? Whatever the reason, no one ever saw it again.

Next time as you are traveling on any of the roads in Virginia and a black dog comes up to you, don't pet it. Your hand just might go right through it!

Chapter Nine
One Girl's Sad Tale
—Gloucester

The tale I am about to tell has all the makings of a story that Edgar Allan Poe might have dreamed up, except he didn't.

In Gloucester, there's a house called Church Hill. In 1650, Mordecai Cooke received a grant of 1,174 acres of land. In 1658, he built a brick house on the site and it became known as Mordecai's Mount. Sometime in the 1700s, the house caught on fire and left only a brick wing. Much later, this part burned, too, and a new frame house was built over the site, becoming Church Hill. The property was inherited by the Throckmortons, descendents of Cooke.

One of these descendents was Elizabeth Throckmorton. The weird part about this is there seems to be no record of her. Whoever the girl truly was, her father took her to London, and it was while there that she fell in love. The object of her affections was an English gentleman. Both declared eternal faithfulness to one another and they promised to correspond by mail to plan their wedding. Dead set against the match, her father intercepted the mail and made sure she never heard from her young man. Not long after, Elizabeth fell ill and died. The story goes on to say because she pined for him, that she lost the will to live. One windy day in November, they buried her in the family graveyard.

There is one weird account that the family butler, angry from some slight done to him by the family, dug up her coffin that very night, hoping to steal any jewels buried with her. But when he tried to remove one ring off a finger, he couldn't. So he cut the finger off.

Not really dead, but in a catatonic state, she revived from the pain of her finger being cut off. Frightened, the servant bolted, never to be heard from again.

Barefoot and dressed in a thin gown, Elizabeth crawled out of the grave. At this time a raging snow storm came up. Managing to stand up, she walked out of the graveyard and toward the house. She reached the front door, but when she scratched at it, no one heard her feeble attempts.

They found her frozen body the next morning, blanketed by snow. A trail of bloody footprints led from the garden—somehow not erased by the snowstorm the night before.

After that, when the first snowfall of the year happened, it is said that sounds of rustling skirts ascending the staircase can be heard, followed by logs being placed in the fireplaces in the house, and then fire crackling from them. When investigated, not one log or fire is found in any of the fireplaces. Also, traces of blood are said to be seen in the pristine snow, a trail from the graveyard to the house. Is this the spirit of the girl seeking to make herself warm, having died freezing to death?

Another weird incident was the time one Julius Browne Jr. rode past the place on horseback and saw the place blazed with lights, even though he knew that the owner, Professor Warner Taliaferro, wasn't at home. He assumed that maybe his sisters might have taken shelter there, since they hadn't gotten home yet, and he went to check it out. His sisters were not there, nor anyone else. Servants from their living quarters on the property also thought that Professor Taliaferro had returned home. He hadn't.

The last bizarre part of this tale is the violets that grow more beautiful and lush near the steps to Church Hill than anywhere else on the property. It is said that maybe the dying girl's tears had fallen on the snow in those spots, tears that gave life to beauty in sadness.

Chapter Ten
The Black Thing of Fort Story—Virginia Beach

This story came to me from my friend David Hawk. The incident happened to his mother, uncle, and a friend of theirs back in the early 1940s.

Fort Story is an Army base located on the lower Chesapeake Bay and Atlantic Ocean in southeast Virginia. It is northeast of the city of Virginia Beach and has been there for at least a hundred years. Today, it is a sub-installation of Fort Eustis, home of the U. S. Army's Transportation Corps. In the forties, Fort Story didn't have a fence surrounding it like it does today. Young people back then would drive their cars around the lonely back roads of the base.

Aleatha Perry, her brother, Herman, and their friend, Eddie, happened to be cruising on Fort Story one night. Suddenly, they saw a flash of shiny black in the car's headlights. Herman whipped the car around. This time, slowing down, they searched for it. It was bobbing along the side of the road.

Herman said, "I am going to find out what that is." He turned the car around once again.

But though they drove the entire length of the road, they never saw the thing again. Spooked, Eddie begged them to take him home. They did and waited until he went inside his home before they left.

David's mother had described it to him as about four feet tall, shiny black, like wet rubber, and looked almost like a kid wearing a sheet for Halloween.

What did they see that night? A shadow person, as paranormal investigators named spirits that look like black shadows? Or some kind of monster? The guards that stand duty at both Gate 1 and Gate 2 have never seen anything. No one will ever know and so the shadow creature joins the other legends of Virginia.

A road on Fort Story—only place where photos were allowed, as it is a military base.

Chapter Eleven
Blood Stain—Richmond, Charles City, Staunton, and Abingdon

There are buildings in Virginia that have a blood stain from another era still on their floors. Like the one at Laser Quest in Shockoe Bottom in Richmond. This building had been a Civil War hospital at one time. Another bloodstain marks the floor of one of the houses on Piney Grove Plantation in Charles City. This stain is all that was left when a woman murdered her husband in bed in another time.

You can still see both stains at these places. Laser Quest's stain is in a room downstairs, beneath the window. The room is to your right as you enter the building.

In the house on Piney Grove Plantation, the stain marks the first floor. Though the murder occurred upstairs, the floor is now downstairs as the current owners used it to replace the first floor that rotted from termites.

There are bloodstains in a foyer of a bed and breakfast in Staunton. They are scrubbed away each night, but return the next morning. They say that these bloodstains came from a Confederate soldier who killed himself when he learned of his wife being unfaithful with a Yankee soldier during the battle of Stanardsville. They say that he still wanders the halls, his pistol in hand to kill the Yankee.

Another blood stain story concerns a young Confederate soldier in Abingdon who had to carry some important papers about the location of the Union army to Robert E. Lee. At the time, he fell in love with a young woman who went to Martha Washington College. To say farewell to his lady love, he traveled through the cave system underlying Abington, snuck up a secret stairway, and entered the college. But just as he joined the young woman, two Union soldiers came up the stairs and discovered them. They fired at him and the soldier fell, his blood staining the floor.

The stain can still be seen today. No longer a college, it is now a hotel, the Martha Washington Inn. Even when carpets are put over it, holes mysteriously appear right over the bloodstains. Even after the floors have been refinished, the stains reappear. It seems that the tragedy will never die there, but stands as a constant reminder of how a war can divide two lovers from each other forever.

Chapter Twelve
Haunting Legends of Virginia Cemeteries

Usually, cemeteries are peaceful, and it is said that ghosts never haunt them, only the places where they frequented in life. Of course, there are many stories of haunted graveyards that disprove this. Myself, I have been in local graveyards in Richmond taking photographs, and getting orbs and misty forms in the finished pictures. Paranormal investigators have taken photos that have similar images and have picked up electronic recordings of whispers from these sites. Some stories I am about to report are true, but still, there are others with unverifiable legends attached to them at these same resting places that can not be proven.

Hollywood Cemetery—Richmond

One interesting thing always said when one was to be buried at Hollywood Cemetery: "You're going to Hollywood" meant you were dying or passed away.

Many famous Virginians are buried here, including Presidents James Monroe and James Tyler. Other famous dead people include Confederate President Jefferson Davis and his family, General J. E. B Stuart, author Ellen Glasgow, and John Randolph. There are many wonderful artworks in the park-like setting such as cast-iron work, angels, and obelisks. While it is a major tourist attraction, Hollywood is still is a working cemetery.

One of the true but bizarre stories about it says that families used to picnic there by the graves of loved ones. Now there a stipulation in the contract for those who seek to buy a grave that no one is allowed to picnic there.

The Confederate Pyramid at Hollywood Cemetery stands guard over countless graves of Civil War soldiers.

Ghostly legends abound in Hollywood Cemetery. One tells of the ninety-foot granite pyramid there, built as a monument to the 18,000 enlisted Confederate soldiers buried near it. In the cornerstone are entombed Confederate artifacts that include a flag, a button from Stonewall Jackson's coat, and a lock of Jefferson Davis's hair. Eleven thousand of the Confederate dead are unknown; many of them brought in from Gettysburg in the 1870s, and interred en masse in Hollywood. Some even came from Belle Isle, where a Union prison had been during the Civil War that buried dead Confederates in a mass grave.

There have been those who've sworn they heard soft moans from these graves at Hollywood on nights when the moon is full. Orbs have been seen floating above tombstones and cold spots felt. There are those of the living whose energy has been drained, leaving them feeling ill the next day. No doubt, the soldiers still want to return home to their loved ones.

Another story involves the statue of a cast iron dog. It came originally from the front of a store on Broad Street in the nineteenth century. A little girl would drop by the store and pet it, talking to it and showing her love for it as if it were a real dog. One day though, she didn't come. The little girl had perished from scarlet fever in an epidemic in 1892, and her family buried her in Hollywood Cemetery. Because of her affection for the cast iron dog, though, they bought it from the store and placed at her grave site. Eerily, it stands there to this very day, as if guarding.

There have been those who say that it moves occasionally, that they would pass it pointing in one direction, and come back to find it staring the opposite way. For me though, it has not moved.

The true story behind the dog is that the Valentine Richmond History Center has in their files a "Letter to the Editor" to the *Richmond Times-Dispatch*. In it, it states the cast iron dog belonged to one Charles R. Reese. Reese's children would walk by the cast iron dog on Broad Street every day and they loved the dog. He bought it for his children and it became a treasured family possession until it was put in the cemetery to prevent being confiscated and reduced to bullets. The cast iron dog does mark the graves of the Reese children.

Not far away is the tomb of famous author Ellen Glasgow. After she passed away, there was a stipulation in her will that her two pet dogs that preceded her in death be dug up from the backyard of

Today, the iron dog did not change positions for me.

her home and buried with her. There are those who claim to hear these two dogs running around and whining at the gravesite, late at night. Could Ellen be tossing them sticks to fetch?

Another legend concerns Richmond's own vampire. You can find his story in the chapter on vampires of Virginia included in this book.

Still another tale involves Thomas Branch, who in 1865, moved his family and business interests from Petersburg to Richmond. He established the Merchants Bank, which is now the Bank of America. He and his sons were such successful financiers that he is considered the "father of Virginia banking."

A statue of a lady stands at his grave. The legend goes that, once a year, she comes to life on the anniversary of his death and sheds tears.

The daughter of President Davis, Winnie, is rumored to have died from a broken heart, caused by her falling in love with a Yankee. The man upon whom she focused her affections, Alfred Wilkinson,

Close-up of the statue who weeps for Thomas Branch.

was the grandson of an abolitionist. President Davis rejected his suit to marry Winnie. Not long after, her health started to fail, and she passed away at age thirty-four. Her father felt that this was due to his denying hers and Alfred's marriage and he'd changed his mind, but it was too late.

A statue of an angel in mourning stands at her grave and it is said that, from time to time, this statue, too, sheds tears, perhaps because even in death Winnie and her lover are still parted.

> Besides a final resting place, Hollywood is also a place you can tour. The cemetery is located at 412 Cherry Street in Richmond. You can find out more about this charming place at http://www.hollywoodcemetery. org/ or call their phone number at 804-648-8501.

A Cemetery in a Shopping Center? —Chesterfield

Little Professor Book Center was once opened in Chesterfield Meadows Shopping Center. When it was still open, the owner, Ron Ferland, told me that someone came into the bookstore and asked him if the gravestones from the Wrexham Hall family plot had not been removed when the land had been sold and the shopping center built. The house itself had been resettled about a block away from its original location. The person thought he had seen the tombstones hidden among the hedges in the shopping center.

This is not true at all, for when I heard the story, I checked and did not see one stone peeking from among the hedges. As for Ron, he never believed the story and never searched for the graves.

I found that the graves had been removed to a cemetery. But to this day, I have heard from others who believe the story of the gravestones being somewhere on the shopping center grounds.

The statue of the angel hovering over Winnie Davis' grave.

The Coffin That Refuses to Stay Close —Petersburg

Blandford Cemetery is in Petersburg. There's a story about a man known as Major Jarvis buried there in a glass-topped coffin, his grave left unfilled so that his wife could view him in repose. But when his wife remarried, she replaced the glass top with a thick marble slab. Legend states that the slab would not stay in place, but tumble to the ground.

But Martha Atkinson, site coordinator for Blandford Church and Cemetery, says she had never seen it out of place.

Does Martin Stand Up in His Grave? —Abingdon

Another story concerns a tomb in Sinking Springs Cemetery that has an unusual mound of stone covered with grass and with an interior iron gate. It is the final resting place of John Henry and Melinda Martin. Both died in the 1890s, and there are supposedly tales that explain why the mound has flourished, though these stories were elusive. It is said, though, that in order to keep an eye on his property on Valley Street, Mr. Martin wanted to be buried standing up. Unfortunately, there has never been any proof to validate that he was buried like this.

The Dog Still Barks—Blacksburg

In Blacksburg, there once lived an African-American who helped his community by hunting and bringing back game to share with the hungry. Every morning he would go out with his beagle. The dog helped with tracking and scared off larger animals such as bear and wildcat. But one day, the old man did not return. When the community went out to search for him, they found both his body and his dog's. Apparently, both had been murdered by someone, though no one had ever been caught or convicted. The man and his dog were buried together in a Blacksburg cemetery on top of a nearby hill.

The legend goes on to say that on the anniversary of the hunter's murder, a dog can be heard barking—sounding exactly like a beagle. Then the dog's barking switches to a long howl as if mourning both their unsolved deaths.

Emory Cemetery—Emory

Strange occurrences have been reported in a cemetery that belongs to Emory and Henry College. As told in *Legends, Stories and Ghostly Tales of Abingdon and Washington County, Virginia* by Donna Akers Warmuth, something peculiar happened to Mr. Brown, a campus security chief at the college. One night, as he patrolled the cemetery as usual, he had just turned his car around in the horseshoe turn, when a fog became blood red and surrounded his car. Frightened, he drove his car out of the cemetery.

There is also a legend about a floating light seen in the graveyard, like someone carrying a lantern. No one has ever seen who it is, whether living or spirit.

Another odd story happened to a female student from the college, one who dabbled in Satanism. She liked to burn crosses in places like this. But one night, she didn't set fire to one; instead, it burst into flames by itself. The girl bolted from the cemetery, not even staying around to put the fire out or see if it went out on its own. There's no conclusion that I could find whether this taught her not to set fire to crosses again, nor is there any evidence whether the story is true.

Next time you attend a funeral or investigate a cemetery, remember not to disturb the dead. Or they may decide to disturb you.

Chapter Thirteen
The Story of Lady Ann Skipwith—Williamsburg

Does she really haunt the George Wythe house, or is Anne Skipwith merely a legend? The line between truth and myth blurs, at least in this interesting tale.

George Wythe was a patriot, Thomas Jefferson's teacher, and the first law professor of the United States. Ann Skipwith's legend begins when she and her husband, Sir Peyton, visited Wythe at his home. Ann was a young woman with a hot temper. When she married, she took up the comfortable life of a planter's wife in Mecklenburg, Virginia. Peyton and she visited the Colonial capital many times, for weeks at a time. This was of course, the norm for those who came to visit towns in those times, as many lived far away from the nearest social gathering. It was during one of these visits, during a gala at the Governor's Palace, that the story goes that the couple had an argument. Ann thought he was consorting with her sister, and she fled in a huff.

As Ann ran toward the Wythe House, she lost one of her slippers. Not pausing to pick it up, she continued until she rushed through the front door of the house and dashed upstairs. The clock struck twelve at that moment. Wearing only one shoe, she made an odd clicking noise all the way up the stairs in that dark and empty house. Which is interesting, for how would anyone know if there's no one in the place at the time? Years later, people would claim to hear that same clicking noise, thinking it was someone with a peg leg. Others claimed it was Ann herself.

The legend becomes even more ingrained with the ghost stories surrounding the house. People speculated that she committed suicide over her husband's infidelities. But like all legends that distort reality, the actual truth is that she died in childbirth in 1779. Peyton did marry her sister, Jean, but not until eight to nine years after her death. Though Peyton and Ann paid extended visits to Wythe House, they never lived there.

The terrible demise of George Wythe, the owner of Wythe House, has spawned a story in itself. Supposedly his grandnephew poisoned him on anticipation of a great inheritance. But it is said that Wythe remained alive long enough to write this nephew out of his will. George did not die in Wythe House though as some believed he did. Instead, he passed away in Richmond in 1806.

Does Lady Ann or George, or maybe someone else, haunt Wythe House? Or is it the sounds of the house settling? In legends, with time, it never really matters. Instead, like such stories, it's perfect to tell on a late autumn evening by the fire, far from the house itself.

Next time, if you visit the Wythe House and hear a clicking noise going up the stairs, ignore it...or not.

Chapter Fourteen
Tales of Two Portraits— Amelia

Haw Branch Plantation is located thirty-five miles southwest of Richmond, in Amelia County. Its particular claim to fame is having more manifestations of psychic phenomena than any of the other haunted houses in Richmond, if not the entire state of Virginia. The mansion is of Georgian-Federal architecture and it derives its name from a small stream on the property, lined with hawthorn trees. For more than two centuries, the place has been a well-known landmark in Amelia County. Set in acres of green lawn, it is surrounded by magnolia and elm trees, and tulips, too.

The most intriguing stories about the place concern two portraits hung there. The first portrait is of a young woman named Florence Wright. Related by marriage to the McConnaugheys who owned the place, not much is known about her. Her parents owned a summer home in Massachusetts and she passed away in her early twenties before the painting had been completed.

The McConnaugheys were told it had been done in color, but when they uncrated it, they found a charcoal rendering. Not one speck of color, just black, dirty white, and gray. They couldn't find the signature of the artist either. They left the back of the frame tightly sealed and hung the portrait over the library fireplace.

A few days later, the sounds of women's voices in conversation would be heard. Gibson McConnaughey rushed upstairs from the English basement of Haw Branch to see who they were. At that time, with the house opened to the public, she assumed it had to be people wanting to view the house. Puzzled, she found no one waiting for her and no car in the parking lot or the road leading away from the house. Throughout the year, five or six times, unexplained voices would echo from the library.

Months later, Cary McConnaughey was reading a newspaper in the library. He happened to look up and saw that the rose in the portrait had started to develop a pinkish tinge, the girl's black hair lightening and the grayish skin changing to the color of flesh. That year, over time, the portrait shifted to pastel colors. Various people from art departments of nearby Virginia colleges had seen it since the time it arrived and acknowledged the metamorphosis to color. They couldn't give any logical explanation for the phenomenon either.

A psychic expert investigated and said that Florence Wright's spirit was tied to the portrait because her death happened before the painting had been completed. It was said that she had the power to leach the color from it if she felt dissatisfied with its hanging spot. But she seemed to like its place at Haw Branch. The psychic said Florence had help from the spirits of two other women. With the return of the portrait's colors, both the changes and the voices stopped.

The previous owner of the portrait, before the McConnaugheys, had claimed that some famous American had painted it, but couldn't remember the name. A year later, the McConnaugheys got their answer. One summer evening in 1972, one of the McConnaughey daughters and her friend sat on the floor of the library beneath the portrait. They stood up and went over to the sofa. At that moment, the portrait did a slow descent down the wall until the frame's bottom crushed a row of porcelain antiques on the mantel shelf, then it tipped forward and flipped over the edge of the mantel. It hit the pine floorboards face down on the same spot the two girls had been earlier, shattering glass all across the floor.

The painting was undamaged, but not the wooden frame. The family found, underneath the backing of the frame ,a brass plate with Florence's full name, her birth date and date of death also. But though they looked it over, they couldn't find the artist's signature. The frame was repaired the next day, new glass put in, and the portrait replaced in it. The man who did the repair tried to find the artist's signature too, but didn't have any success. When they arrived back home with the portrait and took it from their station wagon, Gibson tilted her end of the frame upward. The name J. Wells Champney appeared. Signed in pencil on the apron of the dark mahogany table in the picture, it seemed that only a certain angle of light brought it into sight.

The second portrait is that of a closer relative, Gibson's great-great grandmother, Marianna Elizabeth Tabb. Born at Haw Branch in 1796, Marianna returned there in 1815 as bride to William Jones Barksdale. Her portrait was painted around the time of her marriage and hung at Haw Branch for years. Later, the Barksdales moved to another Tabb plantation, Clay Hill, and spent their remaining years there. Marianna died in 1856, and in January 1861, Clay Hill burned to the ground. Saved from the fire, the portrait was cut from the molding used to frame it. After that, it vanished.

About a century later, Gibson McConnaughey saw a copy of a book of pictures from an exhibit of paintings entitled "Makers of Richmond 1737-1860." The exhibit had been held at the Valentine Museum in 1948. Inside the book, she saw the reproduction of Marianna's portrait. It had been listed as the portrait of Jane Craig Stanard, the woman who allegedly inspired Edgar Allan Poe in his famous poem, "To Helen." Gibson knew it was Marianna and not Jane Stanard because of a copy of the original Warrell portrait hung in an exhibit at Longwood College in 1973.

She wrote to the Valentine Museum and told them of the error in identification. The museum had learned that the Warrell portrait had been bought by a Richmond printer, J. H. Whitty, an avid collector of all things Poe. He had been the one who identified the woman in the portrait as Jane Craig Stanard. The museum couldn't find the painting of Marianna portrait. Then the president of the Poe Foundation found Whitty's collection, bought by another Poe follower, William H. Koester of Baltimore, Maryland.

Around that time, another reproduction of Marianna's portrait was published in a biography of Poe, identifying her as Stanard again. But the McConnaugheys, the Poe Foundation, and the Valentine Museum kept searching for the portrait. Koester died in 1964, his painting inherited by his wife and two sons. All of his collection had been sold to the University of Texas.

Gibson McConnaughey wrote to the Koester son telling of the mistaken identity of the woman in the portrait, and asked if they could borrow or buy it. The son sent a reply that his mother wanted to keep it, but if they ever decided to sell it, the McConnaugheys would be contacted.

In June 1976, the McConnaugheys learned that the portrait was to be auctioned off in Baltimore. Listed as the source inspiration to Poe for "To Helen," the auction owner had been informed of the subject's true identity. Though announced only as a rare old painting by Warrell, the brochure still described it as linked to Poe. Gibson stood up when it came up for sale and announced that it was her great-great grandmother, who had absolutely nothing at all to do with Poe. She showed her proof that she'd brought with her. That negated the Poe collectors' bidding action and the McConnaugheys were able to purchase it as merely an old painting. They took it home and hung it up in the drawing room at Haw Branch.

The strangest thing that is connected to this: Most of the paranormal activity at the plantation ceased after the painting's recovery. Had a lot of the hauntings been caused by Marianna herself, and now that her portrait had come home, has she been satisfied?

But that's not all to the story of the two portraits. Poe becomes closely related once again to these stories.

Edgar Allan Poe wrote the short story, "The Oval Portrait." It is about a man who stays the night in a strange chateau. Reading late into the night, he notices a portrait of a young girl on the wall, set in an oval frame. He becomes absorbed by it. The man describes the portrait as having an immortal beauty, with life-like characteristics. It seems that the girl had fallen in love with an artist and married him. She discovered that her husband was already married—to his career.

The artist wanted to do a portrait of his wife and she let him. For days upon days he painted. So absorbed was he in his work that he failed to notice that his wife was withering away in both health and spirit. Smiling without complaint, she continued to sit for him, as she dearly loved him. The artist allowed no one into the turret and so deep into his work, he never saw his wife's rapidly deteriorating health. Finally finished, he stood before it, entranced with it and calls out in a loud voice, "This is indeed life itself!" Then when he turned to his wife, he discovered her dead.

Chapter Fifteen
Stolen Treasure—Goochland

A myth that could have come out of the writings of Edgar Allan Poe is the one concerning the old Waller gold mine in Goochland County.

Like most stories passed down from generation to generation, the details have worn down and the names of the participants have disappeared. The last known version of this tale surfaced in a "Letter to the Editor" of a Richmond newspaper in the 1930s.

Though the old Waller gold mine in Goochland County had been shut down for about three quarters of a century, it had been mined actively in the 1830s and 1840s. At that time, it was considered the richest gold mine in the United States, with rich ore discovered there. Of course, this was years before the famous gold strike by Sutter on the American River near Coloma, California, in 1848. Closed down, it was reopened sometime in the early 1930s.

A two-story high house with gray, weather-beaten boards and gaping doors and windows was not far from the mine. It was this place that was reputed to be haunted in the 1930s. During the heyday of the mine, several employees of Waller Mine lived here.

Legend has it that strange noises could be heard coming from there, especially at night. Sounds like a despairing cry of someone about to pass into the unknown. These wails were apparently so frightening that some people refused to go near the place and others hurried past it.

When the mine was open, not all of those who lived in the house were honest types. One of these dishonest men pocketed a sizable amount of the gold and kept it hidden in some secret spot near the house. Another man who shared the house with him followed him and discovered where he kept his horde. The legend says that a few nights later, occupants of the house awoke to a high-pitched scream from the hoarder's room. When they rushed in, they found him unconscious on the floor, his head bashed in by a blunt instrument. He died, never regaining consciousness. His death was investigated but nothing was detected as to who committed the crime or why, and the murder remained unsolved for years. When it finally ran out of the mother lode, the Waller mine closed and was boarded up. All the employees went off in different directions.

As sometimes happens in cases like this, the other man who had killed the murdered man for his secret treasure met with an accident himself years later and confessed to the crime. He admitted to sneaking into the victim's room that night to kill him. But when he stepped on a creaky board in the floor, the other boarder woke up and asked who was there. That's when the murderer swung down a pole ax upon the man's head. As the victim screamed, the murderer bolted back to his room and hid the pole ax, then joined the others seeking the source of the scream. Later, he buried the ax, and after things settled, dug up the gold and left for the North.

He never got to enjoy his ill-gotten gains, though. He claimed that the dead man haunted him day and night, and that he had suffered, never knowing peace, since he killed the man. But it seems that his confession didn't appease the victim, for strange noises could still be heard decades after the murder. As Goochland County old timers still remark, "He's still searching in vain for his lost treasure."

Chapter Sixteen
Monstrous Creatures

But the Krell forgot one thing . . . Monsters, John, monsters from the id!

~From *Forbidden Planet*

Monsters do exist in Virginia. At least their legends do. Besides the Sasquatch, there are the various vampire and werewolf stories, along with other monsters and fiends that inhabit the mountains, the valleys, rivers, and even off shore in the Atlantic Ocean. Some have been found to be nothing more than commonplace animals. Others could not be identified. Get comfortable and be prepared to learn about the monsters that have made their home in the Old Dominion.

From Murder Victim to Half Human Monster —Springfield

In the 1880s, there's a legend of a Palestinian who immigrated to Springfield, Virginia. The story says that he was brutally tortured and killed in some woods known now as Lake Accotink Park. Some nights, it is said he is heard moaning. On rare occasions, it is also said he takes the form of a half human, half beast with an eye patch.

Moat Monster of Fort Monroe—Hampton

There's an old army base that is still in use today in Hampton. If you take exit 268 off 64, you can find this place by watching for the Fort Monroe or Casemate Museum signs.

Fort Monroe was founded by Captain John Smith. He named it Old Point Comfort and picked out this small piece of land because of its locality. At Old Point Comfort, the colonists were able to see who was entering the James River. As historians know, the colonists of 1607 were involved in a mini war with the Spaniards. Old Point Comfort played a major role for the lookouts. Old Point Comfort went through several names changes. Its final name change came to be Fort Monroe, named after the President, James Monroe. One would think that James Monroe would haunt the base that was named after him, but he doesn't. He is said to haunt an old law office building in Fredericksburg, Virginia.

There are ghost stories abundant about this place, though. Unlike James Monroe, others continue to haunt here, the most famous apparition being at the plantation-style home called Old Quarters Number One. The house is a *Who's Who* list of distinguished spirits. Those like Edgar Allan Poe, U. S. Grant, Lafayette, Jefferson Davis, and Abraham Lincoln, and Captain John Smith, prowl among its walls, along with ordinary ghosts and the luminous lady of Ghost Alley.

The interior of Fort Monroe houses a "moat." This moat protected the heart of Fort Monroe which houses the main living quarters of officers and enlisted alike. It is like a tiny town encased in original stone walls.

There is a story that this moat contains a water monster. This monster is said to be a relative of the Loch Ness Monster of Scotland. The moat monster has been sighted, but no one has been able to determine what it really is.

Could this monster be a relative of Nessie? Or maybe a large sting ray or skate that became trapped in the moat during high tide? More likely, it is just a figment of an overactive imagination of old sea men and soldiers.

The Monster Haunting Highland County —Highland

Something terrorized Highland County at one time. Sounding like a goose in distress, two fire balls were seen and something messed with one young man's hair, scaring him so much that he passed out.

One resident of the area, Mrs. Griffith, was a teenager at the time the thing caused such a ruckus. She didn't believe any of the tales, and with her boyfriend, plus a nine-year-old girl, went one night after church to investigate the truth. The moon shone bright and that made it easy to see. They came to the fence where the young man had had his incident and climbed up to sit upon it.

They heard a noise. It appeared to come from a sinkhole below. The sound seemed to come closer and closer to the fence.

"It's just a sheep under a tree," said her boyfriend.

Out of nowhere, a strong wind shoved them off the fence. The "thing" jumped onto their backs. They couldn't see it, even with the clear moonlight. When it got off of them, they bolted in fright. It seemed to be close on their heels, as they could feel it breathing down the backs of their necks.

Now, when stories are told of the thing, Mrs. Griffith swears on a stack of bibles that it really exists.

Potters Road Monster—Virginia Beach

Terry Skylar of Ghost FIRE Haunts group in the Tidewater region, told me about a monster that prowls Potters Road in Virginia Beach. This strip of road is long, dark, and most of the time, deserted. There's a gentleman's club at one end of it. It is said that if you drive on the road, you must be very careful because a monster might come out of the wooded area to attack you. Sometimes it is described as a very tall bird-like creature; in other stories it is more dog-like, but much bigger and meaner.

Chapter Seventeen
Green-Eyed Monster
—Richmond

In a July 1935 issue of the *Richmond Times-Dispatch*, a haunted house is mentioned. The tale began when a widow, Georgia Douglas, moved into the house at 419 West Main Street, along with her two daughters and two grandchildren. They all retired early after unpacking all day.

But they received no sleep that night. Instead, something tormented them all night long by thumping under the floor. Assuming it to be a stray dog, they ignored the noise for three weeks.

Then, one night at midnight, a knock came at the door. When Mrs. Douglas opened it, she found nothing. She shut the door, but another round of knocking came. When she threw open the door again, this time she saw a creature that looked half dog, half sheep. Frightened, she stood there, unable to move or say anything. She thought that the thing had the face of a bulldog, a sheep's body, foot-long ears that stood straight out and two green eyes.

By and by, this ended up in the newspaper. The article excited the neighbors and they came over, hoping to hear the noise, too. Four men volunteered to go under the house, discovering tracks from something on four feet, about the size of a human hand, with claw marks ten inches long!

Two nights later, 2,000 people surrounded the house, hoping to get a glimpse of the green-eyed monster. Some suggested it was a raccoon, others guessed it to be an opossum, badger, alligator, polecat, bear cubs, a beaver, an otter, owl, even a peacock. Many other kinds of animals were mentioned also. There were those who said it was a spirit in transit.

Fear rose among the crowds and people thought they heard the creature. Ghost hunters crawled under the house and claimed to find a woman's red hat and black pocketbook along with some suspicious bones. The "bones" turned out to be leftovers from hams, chops, roasts, and T-bone steaks.

A story arose that the place had once been a gambling house and bar, and that a man had been killed there in a card game. Mrs. Douglas said she found a strange stain on the floor and no amount of scrubbing eliminated it. Someone told her that human blood could not be washed off.

The crowds became harder to put up with than all the thumping under the floor had ever caused. Neighbors tossed water over the people, hoping that this would make them go away. It didn't. Traps were set, hoping to catch the monster, and realty agents came by to nail a cover over the entrance under the house to prevent possible damage.

Finally, the "monster" was caught, and it turned out to be nothing more than a female possum carrying a set of quintuplets in its pouch.

Chapter Eighteen
Wampus Cat

Throughout the Appalachian region of the American Southeast, the chilling shrieks of the Wampus Cat may be heard in the night. Bloodthirsty monstrosities, they seemed filled with a palpable anger and hatred. Wampus Cats are known to mutilate and butcher entire herds of livestock, not to sate any sort of hunger, but for the pure pleasure of it. Folklore says Wampus Cats were once witches, but were cursed with an unholy, bestial form as punishment for pursuing secrets no one should ever know. And it is rumored that the Wampus Cat is always female.

From a distance, the Wampus Cat has been mistaken as an overly large, grotesque monkey. Sometimes there are those who call it a Devil Monkey. But up close, one can see the horrid truth. The head is something like that of a feline, with baleful red eyes, and slavering jaws. Its body is vaguely anthropoid, and covered in layers of thick, glossy fur. Beneath the layers, something mockingly like that of the human female form is hinted at. The Wampus Cat carries a bushy-tail behind its body, which it swishes angrily. While the monster can walk upright, it prefers to make astonishing leaps using its hind-legs. Both forepaws and hind legs conceal claws that could easily eviscerate a man. The monster is followed by a repugnant odor, a noxious mix of sulfur and an animal in heat. Like the witches of folklore, Wampus Cats hunt in packs of three. A Cat will never be alone, her companions always watching nearby.

A horror author I know, Stephen Mark Rainey, mentioned on his blog about the Wampus Cat myth. He always assumed that it had only existed in Tennessee, until he heard the stories about it being in North Carolina. But it appears that the creature stalks here in Virginia, too.

Its stories are told mainly in the western and southwestern sections of the state.

One story is an old Indian legend. A young Native American woman became suspicious of her husband. He seemed loyal and loving, but she wondered what he was like when away from home. One night she threw the hide of a mountain lion over herself and snuck out to spy on him when he went hunting.

She hid herself when she came upon the hunting party's camp. From her hiding place she listened to the tales the medicine man told the hunters around the fire they had built that night. She saw one of the men creeping toward her and tried to make her escape, but it was too late. And so she was punished for being where she wasn't supposed to be and cursed to become half woman, half cat. She stood on two legs but had the snout and ears of a cat.

The Wampus Cat is said to prowl the hills, looking for animals to steal. It is said that when the moon is full, you will hear her howl. If you're camping in the woods and hear her piercing wail, beware. She may hunt you.

In another tale, a witch attempts to shapeshift into a cat when local villagers catch her. She flees, doomed to be half cat, half woman forever.

Whatever the truth is, farmers still tell of their cattle disappearing, never to be found, or dying mysteriously.

And the Wampus Cat is blamed for it all.

Chapter Nineteen
Mothman's Appearance in
Virginia—Prince William

The Mothman is a being seen in West Virginia, around Charleston and Point Pleasant, mainly between November 12, 1966 (near Clendenin), and December 1967. For thirteen months, the entire town of Point Pleasant, West Virginia lived in a grip of dark terror culminating in a tragedy that made headlines all over the world.

Most observers describe the creature involved as a winged creature the size of a man, with reflective red eyes and large moth-like wings. The creature often appeared to have no head, with its eyes set into its chest. A number of hypotheses have been presented to explain eyewitness accounts, ranging from misidentification and coincidence to paranormal phenomena and conspiracy theories.

It all began on November 12, 1966, when two young married couples from Point Pleasant, David and Linda Scarberry and Steve and Mary Mallette, traveled late at night in the Scarberrys' car. They had just passed the West Virginia Ordnance Works, an abandoned World War II TNT factory. They noticed two red lights in the shadows next to an old generator plant near the factory gate. Stopping the car, they discovered that the lights were actually the glowing red eyes of a large animal. Shaped like a man, but bigger, it stood maybe six and a half to seven feet tall, with wings folded against its back. Terrified, they raced toward Route 62, where the creature supposedly pursued them at speeds exceeding a hundred miles per hour. From then on, others ran into this monster until the December 15, 1967 collapse of the Silver Bridge spanning the Ohio River.

There are claims that Mothman is related to parapsychological events in the area, including UFO activity, men in black encounters, poltergeist activity, Bigfoot and black panther sightings, animal and human mutilations, and precognitions by witnesses.

One of the early theories is that the Mothman was a misidentified Sandhill crane, which, in the late 1960s, had been a problem in the surrounding area. Sandhill cranes can reach a height of six feet, achieve wingspans of ten feet, have the general appearance described, glide for long distances without flapping, and have an unusual shriek. Other theories suggested the possibility of the Mothman being a barn owl or perhaps a large Snowy Owl. Skeptics suggest that the Mothman's "glowing eyes" are actually *red-eye* caused from the reflection of light, from flashlights, or other light sources that witnesses may have had with them.

Now what does this have to do with Virginia? It seems that the state had its own Mothman experience. One Arlington businessman was in the company of three friends during the winter of 1968-69 in Prince William County. On a farm near Haymarket, they heard a peculiar noise and decided to investigate it. Horrified, they found a large creature with red-orange eyeballs and with wings. They bolted, not looking back.

Today, there is still fascination with the Mothman. In Point Pleasant, West Virginia there's even a museum for it. You can find the museum's Web site at http://www.mothmanmuseum.com/. I've even heard that the *Paranormal State* TV show may be paying a visit. There are even references in books and online of similarities between the Mothman and the Thunderbird of Native American legend.

So the next time you're driving at night, whether in West Virginia or Virginia, and you see something by the side of the road with glowing red eyes, don't stop to find out what it is. Just keep on driving and don't look back. Otherwise, you might find the Mothman flying after you.

Chapter Twenty
Giant Thunderbird
—Louisa County

If you've ever read Indian myths, then you've heard of the thunderbird. It is described as a large bird, capable of creating storms and thunders while it flies. Clouds are pulled together by its wing beats, the sound of thunder is made by its wings clapping, lightning flashes come from its eyes when it blinks, and individual lightning bolts are made by the glowing snakes that it carries with it. In masks, it is depicted as many-colored, with two curling horns, and, often, teeth within its beak. The Lakota name for the Thunderbird is Wakíyą, a word formed from kiyą́, meaning "winged," and wakhą́, "sacred." The Kwakwaka'wakw has many names for the Thunderbird and the Nuu-chah-nulth gave it the name of Kw-Uhnx-Wa. The Ojibwa word for a thunderbird that is closely associated with thunder is *animikii*, while large thunderous birds are known as *binesi*.

Although associated most of the time with the Plains Indians, the Thunderbird was also known to the Algonquin-speaking peoples. However, like most Native American cultures on the East Coast (except maybe Iroquois), little is now known of their beliefs.

In regards to the Thunderbird, this much is known: This fearsome being that resembles a winged man or an immense bird causes fear and dread. The myths tell that it is known to actually kill and eat humans from time to time.

There once existed a gigantic bird in North America. Called the Teratornis Merriami, it stood five feet tall and had a wingspan of twenty-four feet and had the long narrow beak of the predator bird, too. Bones of this bird and humans have been found in the same areas together. Maybe the ancestors of the Native Americans today killed these giant birds for their feathers or myths of the Thunderbird arose due to the birds kidnapping their children and stock.

A possible thunderbird story set in Virginia happened in late 1990s or 2000. A man spied a large bird that flapped its way toward a tree on his land. Being very large and obviously heavy, the tree snapped under it and it went from tree to tree until it finally found one sturdy enough to hold it. He decided to sketch a picture of the bird and drew as close to what the bird looked like as he could. The bird hissed like a goose at him, but he managed to get the picture done. It took off and flew away. He never saw it again. He just knew it was not a vulture or an eagle.

Was this a thunderbird, or just a giant-sized eagle? I searched everywhere I could think of, but could never find the picture this man supposedly drew. Did he keep it?

Whatever it might be, keep your eyes to the sky for maybe you will see this immense bird taking wing.

Chapter Twenty-One
Sasquatch in Virginia

Sasquatch, or Bigfoot, as humankind likes to call them, is supposedly seen only in the State of Washington, maybe even Oregon, Northern California, and other parts of the Far West. But that is wrong, for there have been sightings of Big Foot for more than four hundred years in many other states too, especially in Virginia. The sightings in Virginia would be the oldest sightings, some dating before the 1800s. The Department of Forestry's Web site says there are 15.8 million acres of forest in the state. And with sixty-two per cent of Virginia covered with forest, much of it owned by private citizens, one can believe in the Sasquatch roaming the Commonwealth.

Similar to Asia's Abominable Snowman, the history of Bigfoot reaches far back into America's past with the Indian people. In the Northwest and west of the Rockies, Bigfoot is seen as a special being, all due to close relationship with humankind. Indian tribe elders see him as a border between animal-style consciousness and human-style consciousness, one that gives him special powers. In Indian culture, animals are not looked upon as inferior to humans. Instead, they are regarded as elder brothers and teachers of humans. Interestingly enough, the Northwestern tribes never considered the Sasquatch as other than a physical being. But to other tribes in the U.S., Bigfoot is perceived more as a supernatural or spirit individual. An appearance to humans is meant to convey some sort of message.

The Sioux called Bigfoot Chiye-tanka. Turtle Mountain Ojibwe call the Sasquatch Rugaru, close to the French word, *loup-garou*, which means werewolf. They also associate Bigfoot with Windago, the cannibal-giant of their legends. The Hopi see Bigfoot as a messenger who appears in times of evil.

Among the Iroquois, mentioned much more often than Bigfoot, are the "little people"—both are regarded as spiritual or interdimensional. These are the Pukwudgies. They believe that these beings can enter or leave our physical dimension whenever they wish to. Strange that these little people myths are all over the world, like the little people known as fairies in Europe, for example.

Sightings of the Sasquatch have been reported to this day, even by credible people. To many, these facts suggest maybe the presence of an animal, probably a primate that exists today in very low population densities. Bi-pedal, unlike an ape, it walks with long strides and has a cone shape for the top of the head. If it does remain in lowly populated areas, it has become very adept at avoiding human contact through a process of natural selection.

To others, these same facts point to a cultural phenomenon kept alive today through a combination of the misidentification of known animals (like bears), wishful thinking, and the deliberate fabrication of evidence. Like the video on YouTube at http://www.cryptomundo.com/bigfoot-report/va-bf-video2-2/. Watching it, I admitted how fake it looked right off the bat. That doesn't mean that stories from honest people and Sasquatch investigators aren't real, or that stories told by Indians in the past couldn't be. As with all legendary monsters, there are always those willing to add to the myth on purpose to try to bamboozle the public.

Various Web sites, blogs, and books have pinpointed sightings all over the state, from areas near Washington, D. C. to the Shenandoah Valley, spreading over to the far western part of the state, from Roanoke to Richmond and its counties, as far south as the North Carolina border, and as far east as the Tidewater region.

Hunters who hunt deer and other animals and birds in Virginia have run into Bigfoot. Why hasn't one tried to bag it? One almost did, but when the hunter stared at the six to seven foot creature through his scope, it turned to look at him and he couldn't shoot it, claiming that it looked too human to him.

Another hunter had shot a deer. When he went to grab a knife and came back, he found a Bigfoot, the carcass of his deer under its arm. It gave off a smell not unlike a cesspool that wafted to him even after it took off. This story of taking the man's deer has me wondering, does the Sasquatch eat vegetation, or is this proof that it may consume meat?

There are those who, like ghost hunters, are out to prove the big, hairy apeman's existence and even get legislation pushed to protect the forested areas Bigfoot lives in. And, like paranormal investigators, they use digital cameras, cameras with thermal imaging, and other assorted equipment to collect their proof. There are Web sites online of these Sasquatch hunters, like the Sasquatch Watch of Virginia at http://www.sasquatchwatch.net. There's the Virginia Bigfoot Research Organization where you can find information at http://user1043825. wx15.registeredsite.com/indexhi.htm.

Bigfoot is still being seen in Virginia today. One story involves a female witness who admitted to seeing a Sasquatch twice: One of the times she almost hit it with her car. Another person saw one on Memorial Day, in Chesterfield County at night. That witness was driving when he saw a deer running from a field in front of his car, about fifteen to twenty feet away. Suddenly, some large, hairy creature came out of nowhere and grabbed the deer, carrying it away. Not believing his eyes, the driver screeched to a stop, parked the car, and got out. Not long after, maybe the same creature, maybe not, emerged out of the woods, looked around and motioned for a smaller version to join it. The only difference in the little one from the larger one was in the color of its fur, which was silvery-gray. Both creatures headed off, possibly to search for food in a nearby subdivision. Not the only sighting in Chesterfield County, Bigfoot has been seen in Lake Chesdin in Chester and at Pocahontas Park in Chesterfield, too.

Another witness saw something one night when she heard her two dogs begin to bark. Stepping out onto her deck, she didn't see anything—not at first. Then, as she shined her flashlight toward a small creek, she noticed the crouched silhouette. After she yelled at it, it stood up to seven foot tall. The witness never saw any of its features, but its eyes shone in the light from her flashlight, just like some predator's would. It took off, splashing up creek. The witness claimed it was not a bear or a deer, for it remained upright like a man as it stalked away.

There have been "Skunk Ape" sightings from the swamps of Louisiana and Georgia to the Great Dismal Swamp in Chesapeake in Virginia's Tidewater area. The Dismal Swamp has a haunting beauty. It is a geological wonder and all kinds of reptiles, large and small

Pocahontas Park has had Bigfoot sightings as have other areas of Chesterfield County.

mammals, birds, flowers, giant trees, and beautiful ferns inhabit it. One can believe that the Sasquatch might also exist there.

In 2000, a camp counselor left twelve sleeping campers with her co-counselor and went to take a shower. At eleven pm, everyone was asleep or inside their cabins, preparing to do so. Suddenly, a sound erupted from the wooded area west of the bunk house. At first, she wondered if it was some of the others playing around. But the sound seemed to be coming from one individual—it was a loud howl that morphed into a type of whining bark that ended almost like a hoot. This puzzled her because, although knowledgeable in the sounds of wildlife, she had never heard anything like it. It was an impossible sound for a human to make, yet it sounded so eerily human-like.

The young woman left the circle of light that came from the shower building and headed back to the cabins. Her cabin happened to be the last one and there were no porch lights on. None of this bothered her, until the noise rent the air again. Much closer and much louder too, it frightened her. She walked faster. The howl repeated itself, sounding as if whatever it was had drawn closer, parallel to her path. The young woman broke into a run, and after reaching her cabin, entered it and locked the door behind her. She didn't hear anything else after she got inside, but that may be due to the fact that she put on her Discman to calm herself down and drown anything else out.

Another sighting concerned a man and his wife. They had been walking the Great Dismal Trail for one mile when they sat down at one of the benches they found. As they did so, they heard what sounded like someone walking parallel to the canal on the other side. It sounded like leaves being crunched underfoot and twigs snapping, as if by a two-legged man. Five minutes later, the sounds ended in front of them. Then they started hearing steps coming from the left side, and they listened as both seemed to intercept each other. A couple minutes later, chattering erupted from the center point and to their left. Freaked out, the man used a small, thick pine branch and hit it against a mile marker post a couple of times to see what would happen. Ten to fifteen seconds later, the man and his wife heard a similar banging coming from the area of the footsteps, except deeper into the woods.

The canal is about forty or fifty feet across and very deep; the brush on the other side is dense like a thick wall. Unable to see what made the sounds, the man thought it might be best if he and his wife left. But his wife wanted to see what it was, so they headed back the way they had come from. They found a park ranger in his vehicle waiting to close the gates. As he knew of frequent black bear sightings in this area, the husband inquired how bears might make sounds in the wild. He described the chattering and asked if the bears could do that. The ranger said he didn't think bears produced that sort of sound. They talked a little more, then the man and his wife left the ranger and made for their car. But when they were only twenty feet away from the car, they heard a loud but short scream from the direction of the swamp. It sounded like a cross between a whoop and a woman's scream.

I was there to take pictures for this book, but my husband stayed in the car as I took the boardwalk trail into the woods. We couldn't drive up to Lake Drummond at this time as the fires the park had since late spring were still going on in the swamp. I passed some people heading back to the parking lot, but soon found myself alone. Something about the eerie place creeped me out, like I was being watched. Could it be the spirits that haunt this area? But then

It is easy to imagine a Sasquatch watching you as you walk this path in Great Dismal Swamp.

I thought of Bigfoot and quickly took some pictures, and got out of there, rushing back to my husband and our car.

Not in the swamp, but still in Virginia Beach, a Bigfoot has been reported by three people. They were looking for fish and frogs in a pond when something jumped off a log 200 yards away and screamed. They reported that it ran on two legs. In Seashore State Park, a Bigfoot has been seen near the water's edge. The witnesses said the rangers there told them that they had seen the creatures before, but kept it from the public.

Other sightings have occurred in the western portion of Virginia and down south by the border that divides Virginia from North Carolina. Farmers, hunters, and other witnesses say that Bigfoot walks bi-pedal. Its fur color ranges from reddish-brown to silvery-gray. By many accounts, it stands from four feet to nine feet in height—many witnesses smell a terrible odor, too. Unlike the one hunter mentioned earlier in the chapter who couldn't shoot it, other hunters had no compunction about firing their guns. One hunter was pretty sure he hit it once after shooting at it three times. But there is no mention by this hunter in the story I found online advising whether he ever recovered a body or discovered any blood.

In an old family story, the nephew of one man who returned from Vietnam told how his uncle sat on the porch of his mother's house and saw out of the corner of his eye what he thought was a man. Thinking it to be a neighbor, he told the neighbor to come on up. Then he realized that the man stood at chest height with the porch. The porch was a good six feet off the ground and that would make the man maybe nine feet tall. He also realized the man was covered in hair. The "monkey man or bear man" as he called the creature, leaped onto the porch. Just then his mother came out and he shoved her back inside, joining her. Doors locked, chairs lodged against them, and the windows shades drawn, he stayed up all night, afraid that the thing would return. It never did.

Two other sightings of the creature's appearance have been reported in the area. One was by two young girls, another by a man who claimed that it killed some of his hunting dogs in their dog lot one evening.

Another tale came from a woman whose ex-husband's family owned a cattle farm in Fauquier County, where one evening, as she chatted with her sister-in-law and the sister-in-law's husband outside, they heard a loud wail. Maybe a half mile off to the south or south east of their driveway, the noise came again, two or three more times. The man had been a hunter for a long time and the sister-in-law grew up on the property, and neither had heard a sound like this before. The witness has a sister who worked for the National Zoo in Washington, D.C., and the witness also had not heard anything like the sound at the zoo—ever. Deep and throaty, as if from a large-chested animal, whatever it was, sounded neither threatening nor a plea for help. In the length of time the witness lived there, she never heard it again.

A Bigfoot encounter was reported in a nearby Civil War battlefield in Richmond recently. According to that account, a Civil War reenactment was taking place when one of the soldiers saw the creature. He believed it was a devil, because of the red eyes. Taking aim, he shot at it and the creature let out a loud moaning noise. It bolted into the woods.

The next tale happened in 2005 at Varina, which is located in Henrico County. The witnesses were a woman, her sixteen-year-old son, her son's nineteen-year-old girlfriend, and another twenty-one-year-old boy. The incident occurred in a forest with a creek that ran through it. The creek had some banks as high as twelve feet. The sighting occurred immediately after a bad storm, at midnight, in the spring time. The moon shone bright, which aided in the sighting.

The woman was driving with the others in the car when she saw the creature squatting by the creek. When it saw it was being observed it left the area and went onto the road. She drove away and stayed out of its view for fifteen to twenty minutes. Then she drove back, and she saw that it had returned to the creek and was standing next to it. It looked up at them and she drove off again.

The same site is known for its Indian burial grounds, with a Civil War Battlefield a mile away.

In Pulaski County, in July 2006, a man sighted a Bigfoot in Claytor State Park. The nearby interstate and US 11 follow closely the old Wilderness Road, a footpath and wagon trail for settlers traveling south down the Shenandoah and Roanoke valleys from Pennsylvania. This was hundreds of years before European pioneers started streaming down the valley in the mid-1700s. The road had been a well-traveled hunting and raiding route used by southern Cherokee and Catawba tribes, as well as members of the northern Iroquois Confederacy of Five Nations. Later, a mystic German sect called the Ephrata Brethren (later to be known as Dunkard's) decided the land now covered by Claytor Lake was the place they wanted to stop. When the New River was dammed to form Claytor Lake for the generating of electric power in 1939, the community known as Dunkard's Bottom was swallowed by the rising waters.

The witness sailed his boat into a cove area to do some fishing. As he fished, a sound reached his ears from off the edge of the lake bank. It sounded like three low grunts. Next he heard the noise of something crashing through the woods and up a hill. No doubt he thought it was a deer or bear and resumed his fishing. A few minutes later, sounds of tree limbs snapping and breaking reached him and then a large, heavy boulder flew out of the woods and splashed in the lake about fifty yards in front of his boat. Feeling unwelcome and frightened, the man got away from the area as quick as he could.

In Buchanan County, a Bigfoot was seen hovering around a garage, then it disappeared. This took place in a hollow in the mountains that had plenty of people living there. Later, the nephew of the witness talked to a friend who heard some noises and grabbed a gun. The friend admitted that he shot at something, most likely a bear. That night as the friend slept, something roared outside, and he went out and spied something human looking, standing about five feet tall. He shot at it but missed. He found tracks and examining them, saw five toes and that the print was as big as his own.

There is one last Web site of Bigfoot encounters I like to mention, that covers sightings from state to state. The link is http://www.bigfootencounters.com/. As it says on the main page of the site, it has been put together by "many wonderful people including scientists, friends, forestry, fish and game, loggers, USGS workers, Native Americans, First Nation Canadians, the Chinese, Mongolians, Russians, Tibetans, Indonesian scholars, trackers, guides, coolies, porters, translators and skilled laymen." The Web site is wonderful and covers classic stories of Bigfoot across the nation to current reports, theories, hoaxes, and more.

I also got to interview Billy Willard of SasquatchWatch.Net on what a Sasquatch researcher and hunter does.

Billy Willard

Have you seen a Sasquatch yourself?

No, I have not. However, two of my sons did have a sighting on private property in Varina, Virginia. They described it as gray/silver in color, with dirty, matted hair, very large and broad with a head shaped like a dome, and it stood approximately eight to nine feet tall. Their sighting lasted for about two to three minutes, but they had gotten a good look at it. It was approximately eighty feet away from them. The logo on my Web site at www.sasquatchwatch.net is an artist's rendition of what they saw. Two very close friends of mine have also had sightings.

What is the most harrowing experience you've had while doing these investigations?

Wow, there have been a few, but I would have to say during the time my two sons had their sighting. At the time, Tom Lancaster and I were in the woods below their location, probably near a stream about a hundred yards away. We were walking through the woods to possibly flush something out at the time. When they notified us on the phone that they were having a sighting, my partner, Tom Lancaster, immediately exited the woods into their direction, leaving me alone in the woods. I continued my venture up the stream and suddenly, about a minute later, I became strangely disoriented. I can't explain why because it's never happened to me before or since then. A feeling came over me to where I felt I didn't want to continue and I simply lay down on the ground. I even had a very sick feeling, a nausea-type feeling. After about a minute or so of that, I got my senses back and made my way back out of the woods and was fine. During my travel out though, I did catch a glimpse of "something" quickly moving from left to right in my peripheral vision. What it was, I don't know. I can only assume that it was the creature that my sons had seen.

Which experience has been the most wonderful one—the one you could say gave proof?

Well, it depends on what is considered proof. Science will never accept any eyewitness accounts, photos, videos, prints, etc. . . as proof. Science wants a body unfortunately. The footprints we found, plus the sounds we have heard and the things we have seen are good enough for me.

One experience that I had but I have not talked about very much is an encounter that didn't happen in Virginia, but in Paris, Texas. Tom Lancaster and I were on an expedition there. The last night of our stay, we both had an experience that we will *never* forget. We were camping in a two-room tent. My cot was up at the front of the tent and Tom's mattress at the rear of the tent. The last night of the expedition Tom heard something large walk up to our tent, sometime after 3 am. I was asleep during this time. He saw a large shadow silhouette of something standing outside. He saw a large hand rub on the tent and then whatever it was, grabbed the tent poles on the outside of the tent and shook them violently. Afterwards, things grew quiet. Now, in the meantime, wore out, I slept through all of this. Tom heard me snoring loud in the front of the tent as I have severe sleep apnea. All of a sudden, he heard me snore and then something outside imitate my snoring!

Later, something happened that woke me up. My cot nestled against one side of the tent, and a part of my leg and knee poked into the tent fabric. I woke up to something grabbing hold of my leg right above my knee, squeezing pretty hard. I reached out to grab whatever it was; but my hand couldn't fit around it. I brought up my second hand and wrapped both of my hands around what felt like a hairy wrist. I tried to pull off whatever had a hold of me, but I couldn't. Desperate, I balled my hand into a fist and hit it. It let go of me then. Things became silent outside and I thought I had just had a bad dream and went back to sleep.

When we woke up, I started to tell Tom about the dream when he stopped me and told me about what he had experienced. It was at that point that I realized I didn't have a dream. As I got up, I noticed my leg felt sore. I looked at it and saw that it was red right above my knee. That sort of sunk in the reality of what had happened. Tom and I both kept this quiet for a long time but it is something neither of us will ever forget.

How long have you been doing this?

My son, Josh, and I started Sasquatch Watch of Virginia in 2004. I have always been interested in the Bigfoot/Sasquatch phenomenon, but didn't actively start researching it until four years ago.

How do you collect evidence of Bigfoot, and what do you do with it?

Depends on the type of evidence we find. A footprint will be documented by photos and if it's good enough, we will cast it with plaster. Evidence such as tree structures, stick structure, and formations are documented by photos and GPS marking coordinates to overlay on a mapping program. If any hair is found, it is immediately collected, placed in a paper bag or envelope and sent to a certified laboratory for analysis. We haven't been lucky enough to find a hair sample, but a close friend of ours has. This research takes a lot of time and patience. You don't find something every time you go out. If you did, that would create a lot more questions than answers in my opinion. There are many more times that we find nothing than finding anything of value.

Name some areas in Virginia where the Sasquatch has been seen the most. Also the least seen.

The most would be Montgomery County, Pittsylvania County, Culpeper County, Chesterfield County, Franklin County, and believe it or not, Prince William County near the Quantico Marine Base. The least...the rest of the counties have had less than two sightings in several years. There have been over hundred sightings in Virginia that have been documented in some way or another. For some reason, there was an increase in sighting activity during 2006. There were a total of ten documented sightings in Virginia alone that year.

Where are the most frequented areas Bigfoot has been seen or heard in Virginia?

Right now, Culpeper County. There have been very recent encounters and vocalizations heard. We are currently investigating areas of Culpeper/Fauquier County due to the reports. We can't reveal exact locations due to private property owner requests and active investigation reasons.

I saw that you're a Sasquatch investigator for the State/Commonwealth—what do you do for them?

We are actively pursuing research in Virginia, but we don't do work for Virginia; just do active research in the state. Using our Web site, we try to catch folks in Virginia to send us reports of their encounters.

Can you give us your own theory what the Sasquatch might be? Do you believe Bigfoot to be intelligent or another species of ape?

My own personal theory is that it is an undiscovered primate. Now, keep in mind, we as humans are also considered primates. So, could I accept the idea that they are some type of ancient human? Sure. But, I think the more logical explanation is that it is simply a North American ape of some sort. Intelligent? Yes! These creatures seem to be very smart, enough to remain elusive of humans for all these years. We have to ask ourselves this. Do they remain elusive because of what they have seen humans do to one another all these years—like kill each other with weapons, fight, and make war? It makes you wonder.

Name some of the more interesting stories behind your investigations.

I will give you some Web site links to some of our investigations with names and stories:

http://sasquatchwatchdatabase.blogspot.
            com/2007/11/pulaski-county.html.
http://sasquatchwatchdatabase.blogspot.
            com/2007/09/henrico-county.html.
http://sasquatchwatchdatabase.blogspot.
            com/2007/09/fauquier-county.html.
http://www.teamnesra.net/drupal/?q=node/135.
http://teamnesra.net/drupal/?q=node/188.

Has anyone in the areas you've investigated mentioned any myths behind the Sasquatch—like any of the Native American tribes, for example? (Especially as they are in many myths of Northwestern Indians, Hopi and Iroquois.)

No, but I sure wish I could find some Native Americans in Virginia willing to discuss their stories. I believe the Native Americans have a lot of additional insight into this mystery. You can email me at billywillard@comcast.net with stories.

I have your Web site, but go ahead and give the link again!

The Sasquatch Watch of Virginia Web site can be found at http://www.sasquatchwatch.net.

Tell us about your radio show, Sasquatch Detective. What times is it on? Where can one hear it? And what are some of the shows about?

Sasquatchdetective Radio is a show dedicated to interviewing other Bigfoot researchers as well as eyewitnesses who have had Bigfoot encounters. Sasquatchdetective Radio was the first radio show about Bigfoot on the BlogTalk Radio network. Steve Kulls is the host and I am the co-host. We now have a second co-host by the name of Becky Sawyer. The show is on every Monday night at 9 pm Eastern Standard Time. The show can be found and listened to at http://www.blogtalkradio.com/TheSasquatchDetective. There you will find not only a live link to the shows on Monday, but also all of the archives of shows in the past.

Give any other links you like people to know about and join— like your yahoo group, MySpace. And any other Web site links you like.

Web site: www.sasquatchwatch.net.
Sasquatch Watch of Virginia Forum: http://s9.zetaboards.com/sasquatchwatch/index/.
MySpace: http://www.myspace.com/billywillard.
Yahoo Group: http://tech.groups.yahoo.com/group/sasquatchwatch/.
Facebook: http://www.facebook.com/profile.php?id=1078591383.

The next time when you go hiking in the woods along the Blue Ridge Parkway or among the woods of the Dismal Swamp, or even in the backyard of your own county, keep your eyes open. If you hear a peculiar noise out in your backyard late one night and you peek out the window to see what it is, be careful. For something may be watching you. Something big and hairy.

Chapter Twenty-Two
Werewolves on the Prowl

Werewolves, also known as lycanthropes or wolfmen, are mythological humans with the ability to shapeshift into wolves or wolf-like creatures. This can be either by being bitten by another werewolf or from being placed under a curse. The medieval chronicler Gervase of Tilbury associated the transformation with the appearance of the full moon; however, there is evidence that the association existed among the ancient Greeks, appearing in the writings of Petronius. Shape-shifters similar to werewolves are common in tales from all over the world, though most of them involve animal forms other than wolves.

There are traits that only a werewolf has. Like the joining of both eyebrows at the bridge of the nose. Other indicators are curved fingernails, low set ears, and a swinging stride. One method of identifying a werewolf in its human form was to cut the flesh of the accused, under the pretence that fur would be seen within the wound. A Russian superstition tells that a werewolf can be recognized by bristles underneath the tongue.

The appearance of a werewolf in its animal form varies from culture to culture, though they are most commonly portrayed as being indistinguishable from ordinary wolves save for the fact that they have no tail—a trait thought characteristic of witches in animal form. They also retain human eyes and voice. After returning to their human forms, werewolves are usually documented as becoming weak, debilitated, and undergoing painful nervous depression.

Historical legends describe a wide variety of methods for becoming a werewolf, one of the simplest being the removal of clothing and putting on a belt made of wolf skin, probably as a substitute for the assumption of an entire animal skin (which also is frequently described). In other cases, the body is rubbed with a magic salve. To drink water out of the footprint of the animal in question or to drink from certain enchanted streams were also considered effectual modes of accomplishing metamorphosis. According to Russian lore, a child born on December 24 can become be a werewolf. Folklore and literature also depict that a werewolf can be spawned from two werewolf parents. In Italy, France, and Germany, it is said that a man turns into a werewolf if he, on a certain Wednesday or Friday, goes to sleep outside on a summer night, with the full moon shining directly on his face. In Galician, Portuguese, and Brazilian folklore, it is the seventh son after six sons (though sometimes it can be the seventh child, a boy, after a line of six daughters) who becomes a werewolf. In Portugal, the seventh daughter is supposed to become a witch and the seventh son a werewolf; the seventh son often gets the Christian name "Bento" (meaning "blessed) as this is believed to prevent him from becoming a werewolf later in life. There are also those myths that say that the transformation is accomplished by satanic allegiance, often for the sake of sating a craving for human flesh. And of course, among the Native Americans there are the skinwalker stories.

I found two werewolf legends in Virginia. One takes place during modern times, the other after the Civil War.

The Werewolf of Henrico—Henrico County

There have been sightings of a werewolf in Henrico County. There's no proof that it truly existed, as I could find nothing more on it other than reports circulating about it in stories on the Internet. It is claimed that the monster has been mostly seen in the Highland Springs area, hanging around the Confederate Hills Recreation Center and the Osborn Boat Landing.

Described as having the body of a human and the face of an animal, it runs on all fours or on its hind legs. Standing at six feet tall and covered all in gray or white hair, it has only been seen under the full moon and is harmless except for charging at people.

Of course, the experts in the paranormal say it is most likely a Bigfoot. Still the full moon angle just smacks of a werewolf.

A young man and his girlfriend were enjoying the full moon at Osborn Boat Landing on the park deck, and talking, when they heard some bizarre howls. The noise shocked the girlfriend and when the young man turned, he saw two huge, stocky-built white dogs in the light. The animals lingered for what had to be about ten minutes. Unable to run to their vehicle parked a hundred yards away, the man and his girlfriend stayed there. One of the creatures walked over to the pavilion and leaped onto the picnic table for a few seconds, then jumped off and ran over to his car and checked it out. It took its time as it made its way over to the trees, while the other one remained in the shadows.

Luckily for them, their rescue came as another car drove up. First, one of the creatures howled at the other car, then crashed through

In such a lovely spot as Osborn Landing in the daytime, it's hard to imagine a werewolf prowling there.

the woods. Both the guy and his girlfriend took their chance for escape, hoping the other one wouldn't chase them, and bolted to his car and jumped in. He drove to the other side of the trees and turned the lights on. Neither hide nor hair of either of the "beasts" could be found. He admitted that he will never go back there after dark.

What did he see? Werewolves? Dogs on the loose? Or something else?

Werewolf of Cumberland Gap —Southwestern Tip of Virginia

Some years after the Civil War ended, a legend arose of a werewolf prowling in the mountain forests of the Appalachian Mountains in the southwestern tip of Virginia. Accused of killing sheep and other farm animals, it was even blamed for the mysterious disappearances of several young women in the area. This beast so frightened the locals that they refused to venture outdoors when the full moon moved across the night sky.

A hunter was out hunting when he saw it. Thinking it was an escaped circus animal or a mountain lion, he tried to track it, but it eluded him. Months later, as he slept on a rocky ledge, he woke up and found the creature staring at him. It was the biggest and strangest wolf he had ever seen.

He fired his rifle at it, but the creature got away into some brush. He returned a week later with some bloodhounds to track it, but didn't find any tracks, just a small amount of dried blood. He took a sample to be analyzed. He got his answer back—it was human blood.

Whether wolf or human, the beast was never seen again.

Chapter Twenty-Three
Virginian Vampires
—Richmond, Big Stone
Gap and Port Royal

A legend of the "Richmond Vampire" is connected to the train that is buried under Church Hill and Hollywood Cemetery. The tale began Sunday, October 2, 1925, when tunnel laborers had been digging for Chesapeake and Ohio Railroad. They had decided to build a tunnel through the hill instead of routing the train around Richmond. It was roughly estimated to cost $1.1 million at the time to do so; the objective was to improve rail access to Richmond from the east. When completed, the tunnel would measure around 4,000 feet long, making it one of the longest tunnels in the country at the time. But its usage was short-lived. A cave-in happened as they were digging into the hill and six houses in Jefferson Park collapsed down into it. Some men escaped, but others perished under dirt and rock. The Chesapeake and Ohio Railroad reportedly celebrated its closure and that seemed to be it at the time.

W. W. Poole

With this terrible catastrophe, the vampire tale that came about was that one survivor was actually some kind of fiend that dug his way out of the tunnel. He had been discovered over the body of this one survivor and when he looked up, he revealed a mouth full of jagged teeth. It was said that he ran all the way back to a mausoleum in Hollywood Cemetery pursued by the angry mob. The mausoleum belonged to W. W. Poole.

Some say Poole was called a vampire due to a rare blood disease he had. An accountant in life, he passed away in the early 1920s. The crypt is only marked W. W. Poole, with no birth date, just the year of his death—1922. The date of his death and the date of the train tunnel collapse make it hard to believe that Poole is the vampire, and yet, the legend is recorded in books and by word of mouth that he is the vampire accused.

It is also said that his remains were stolen from the crypt by Satanists and then found. For years after the "vampire" incident, people would try to break into Poole's tomb, to vandalize or sometimes just to stake him. Hollywood Cemetery finally had to remove Poole's body and his wife's, burying both at an undisclosed location. The door to the original tomb was also welded shut.

The truth behind the legend might be attributed in reality to a fireman, Benjamin F. Mosby. Burned almost beyond recognition, he was rushed to Grace Hospital and died twenty-four hours later. He is supposedly the victim the vampire had been found hovering over.

Today, you can visit the cemetery, take a tour of the lovely grounds, and see Poole's mausoleum. And while you're in Richmond, go to Shockoe Bottom and Church Hill to see the infamous hill where a train and bodies are still buried. Just be sure to do this during the daytime. For you never know if the vampire still stalks the night, looking for foolish victims.

Poole, the Richmond vampire is not the only vampire legend in Virginia. There are tales of other blood suckers that make the Commonwealth their home.

A Grave Situation

Over a hundred years ago, some bodies had been resurrected from their graves by grave robbers. But caught at it, they dumped the bodies on the cold earth and escaped. All this was recorded in the *Alexandria Gazette*.

What has this to do with vampires? Well, one of the bodies had two ridges around the wrist of each arm. At the time, for no reason I could find, it was speculated that maybe a vampire and its helpers had been behind the incident.

The tombstone of the Richmond Vampire—W. W. Poole—at Hollywood Cemetery.

Satisfying Hunger

Another vampire legend arose in the Dominion around Big Stone Gap in the 1890s. It all started when a farmer found two of his cattle, slaughtered. Both had been dismembered, the head and hindquarters were all that remained, and they also had been drained of every drop of blood. Not long after, other animals began to be found in the same condition.

A European going by Rupp was the one suspicions centered on. One of many foreigners who came to the area hoping to make a fortune in the mines there, he lived in a cabin in the woods not near any human habitation and was hardly ever seen in town. The suspicion grew when two boys caught sight of him through a cabin window, gnawing on what looked like the raw leg of a cow. People demanded that the sheriff arrest him, but having no proof (and besides, it wasn't against the law to eat raw meat), the sheriff refused.

Weeks later, the town drunk went missing. His body was discovered in the woods a quarter of a mile from Rupp's cabin, drained of blood and missing an arm and leg. Then a second person went missing, a traveling salesman. His body, also missing blood and body parts, was found in the woods not far from Rupp's place.

Vigilantes took matters into their own hands and rushed to Rupp's cabin, armed. They bashed open the unlocked door and stumbled back from the terrible stench that filled the place. Body parts were strewn across the floor. Some of the men had to step back outside to retch.

They never found Rupp. Like some ghost, he had disappeared. They set fire to the cabin and burned it to the ground. A posse searched for Rupp the next day with no results. He had simply vanished off the face of the earth, or at least, that area. To this day though, stories are told in Big Stone Gap of his spectral sightings.

Political Eating

The next vampire legend takes place near Port Royal. One Sir Thomas Lunsford had been accused of being a child eater. An article in the January 1909 issue of *Virginia Historical Magazine* made references to Lunsford being accused of being a real-life vampire.

Born about 1610, Lunsford was a member of an ancient family in Sussex, England. Violent and lawless when young, he tried to kill

Sir Thomas Pelham, a neighbor in 1632. Lucky for Pelham, the balls from Lunsford's pistol missed and Lunsford got sent to jail, which he escaped from later.

A staunch supporter of King Charles, he enlisted in the Army. Eventually, he was given command of a regiment of foot soldiers. In December 1641, he was appointed as lieutenant of the Tower of London. This caused controversy. His enemies stated him as a man of nasty temperament, unfit for the position, that he never attended church, and was of "decayed and desperate fortune." Further accusations had him as being part of a band of murderers formed to assassinate many of the Lords and Commons. There had even been reports that he was a cannibal and ate children. Pictures and caricatures represented him in armor, cutting a child into sections of meat and burning towns and murdering women and children.

Was the man really a vampire or cannibal, or falsely accused? He sided with the king who was opposed by the general populace. The political turmoil of the times, with Puritan beliefs rising high, made such supernatural accusations believable. Look at the witchcraft trials in Salem, Massachusetts, and even in Virginia itself. When King Charles was beheaded in 1649, his followers, in order to escape death themselves, fled the country. One of these was Lunsford, who sought safety in Virginia.

He bought land on the Rappahannock River and built a home near Port Royal and named it Portobago. In England, he was in the center of controversy and labeled a monster. But in Virginia, his life seemed quiet, staying that way until he passed away about 1653.

The next time you go out in the cool Virginian night, make sure you are wearing a cross on a necklace around your neck and are carrying holy water in a vial tucked in a pocket. After all, you never know if Virginia's vampires aren't still seeking the blood of their next victim.

The Appomattox River in Hopewell where Chessie was seen in the 1980s.

Chapter Twenty-Four
Chessie—Chesapeake Bay and Appomattox River in Hopewell

Like Loch Ness and other famous lake monsters and sea serpents around the world, Virginia has its own water beastie. From online stories to the pages of *Weird Virginia* and other books, this creature has made its mark. Chessie is said to live in Chesapeake Bay. For years, people reported sightings of a serpent-like creature with flippers—not unlike Nessie of Loch Ness in that respect. It even made the news in the late 60s.

One witness in a boat said it came out of the water, raising its head. There were fins and something like hard scales on its body. It rose so high that its head could even be seen by the person in the crow's nest. Suddenly, it dove back into the water and, turning around, swam away from the boat, showing all a fanned tail.

In 1978, a retired employee of the CIA claimed to have seen four Chessies off shore, seventy-five yards away. His neighbors even saw them.

Chessie reports kept coming when the 1980s rolled around. No fewer than four charter boats carrying twenty-five people noticed the creature. Witnesses made claims that the creature looked to be maybe about twenty-five to forty feet in length, was dark, with no limbs, fins, or distinguishable details on its oval head. It was also no more than a foot across in width.

One Richmond resident saw Chessie, or something like it, in the Appomattox River in Hopewell in 1980. The witness, a woman, had gone out to dinner with her husband at the Harbor Light Restaurant. The place sat next to the river and when she climbed out of the car, she noticed something strange in the water. It had a long, undulating body and it swam closer and closer. With a reptilian head on a long snake-like body, it matched descriptions of the beast seen in Chesapeake Bay.

Did this creature swim alongside the coast until it got into the mouth of the river and then made its way to the vicinity of Hopewell? Good question.

During May 31, 1982, around 7:30 pm, a couple named Robert and Karen Frew caught sight of an animal in a bay at Love Point, close to the mouth of the Chester River. It swam up to a hundred feet away from them and Robert grabbed a video camera and taped it. It headed toward some swimmers, dove beneath the water, passed underneath the swimmers and came back up on the other side of them. The videotape later showed definitely an animate object and not a log or something else.

The Enigma Project, headed by Michael Frizzell, got a hold of the Frew videotape to show it to George Zug and a group of scientists at the Smithsonian Institution's Museum of Natural History. Sadly, the videotape wasn't good enough for them to determine any conclusions about the "animate" object.

Later in 1994 and 1995, a manatee wandered into the bay. The authorities named it Chessie. They attached a tracking device to it and its seasonal movements into northern waters confirmed that maybe Chessie the sea serpent was nothing more than a manatee. The strange thing about this is how could something like an overweight seal be equated with a thin, snake-like serpent?

The next time you go boating on the Chesapeake Bay and see something suspicious maneuvering in the water that looks like a long snake, don't worry, it's only Chessie.

Chapter Twentieth-Five
Jersey Devil Sighted in Virginia?

The Jersey Devil is a famous legend of the New Jersey Pine Barrens. This creature is so famous that New Jersey's hockey team is called the New Jersey Devils. Deep in the heart of South Jersey, there lies a huge span of dark, desolate woods. These trees give off an eerie feeling—as if you are constantly being watched by someone or something. The plants are so dense that sometimes it is hard to follow a path, and you never know what kind of wildlife is concealed in the brush.

The legend of the Jersey Devil terrorized, puzzled, and intrigued New Jersey's population for over 265 years, since before the birth of our country. It is a mystery that has been passed down from generation to generation and still remains unsolved. Two centuries after the legend's origin, there are still only myths, theories, and horrifying recounts of sightings.

The legend begins in 1735 when a pregnant Mrs. Leeds of Smithville was about to give birth one stormy night. This was to be her thirteenth child, and Mrs. Leeds was feeling old before her time. She cursed the unborn baby during a fit of painful contractions, yelling out, "Let this child be a devil!"

Mrs. Leeds soon forgot her curse when the midwife placed a beautiful baby boy in her arms. Just then, the baby's body began to mutate before her eyes. The baby's face elongated to resemble a cross between a bat and a horse. Long, dark wings sprouted from his shoulder blades. His legs grew long and thin, and his pudgy feet hardened, becoming hoof-like extremities. Fear rose in everyone in the room as long claws sprouted from the baby's fingertips and his blue eyes turned yellow. The beast let out an ear-piercing scream and then it burst through the roof of the cabin, flying off into the night.

Pretty creepy, huh? Just like something out of the *X-Files*, or a scary horror flick. Though that is the most common and widely accepted version of the legend, there are several variations to the tale. To begin with, the name Leeds: There are two names of the Jersey Devil's mother—Mrs. Leeds and Mrs. Shrouds. Historians claim that both a Leeds and a Shrouds lived in the town of the monster's birth. Perhaps the Jersey Devil had been an illegitimate child who was cursed by the townspeople before birth. Though most likely the Devil has a human father, the folks of that time did not believe the Jersey Devil had a human father. They believed the creature to be a product of Satan himself, mixed with human flesh.

There are also several variations on the events of the Jersey Devil's birth. Some say that it was born as a devil and never resembled a human. Other variations claim that before the Jersey Devil flew off into the Pine Barrens, it killed and ate all the people present in the cabin of its birth. It has also been said that for years the Jersey Devil would return to its home and sit perched on a fence. After a while, Mrs. Leeds/Shrouds, not knowing what to do with her deformed child, "shooed" it away, and it took off, never to return.

The first five years after its birth were horrific. The Jersey Devil did so-called "chimney raids" where it would enter a house through the chimney to terrorize the inhabitants. It would allegedly tear up furniture, chase people and pets, and kidnap children by dragging them up the chimney. Its less violent activities included tangling clothes lines, rustling bushes, hovering over lone travelers, and casting strange shadows.

In 1740, one clergyman decided to exorcise the Jersey Devil. The people of the Pine Barrens received instant relief as the sightings suddenly ceased. The legend lived on though, and passed down from generation to generation with a warning that the exorcism would only last for a hundred years. It was warned that those who lived in the Pine Barrens in the 1840s should be prepared for the creature's return. And by the continued stories of its sightings, it seemed that it did indeed return there.

What has this to do with Virginia? It seems that during the period between the 1830s and 1840s, the Jersey Devil decided to visit Virginia. Among its victims were mutilated livestock, dogs, geese, cats, and ducks. It allegedly attempted to grab children in the state as well. The Devil finally left Virginia to reemerge in the Pine Barrens of New Jersey in 1909. During the week from January 16 to the 23rd, it was blamed for the mutilation of livestock and pets, and leaving hoof-like prints in, on, and around houses. Over one thousand people in New Jersey reported encounters with the creature during that time.

What is the Jersey Devil? More important, why at that time in history did it decide to come to Virginia and terrorize the state? These questions may never be answered.

Chapter Twentieth-Six
Chincoteague Ponies
—Chincoteague and Assateague

I would have never thought of the Chincoteague ponies of Assateague Island if not for a friend asking me if I would include their legend in the book. Who hasn't read the bestselling book *Misty of Chincoteague* by Marguerite Henry and wanted a Chincoteague pony for their very own?

A Chincoteague mare and colt at the Chincoteague Pony Center.

Chincoteague ponies run free on the Virginia side of Assateague, a thirty-seven-mile-long barrier island off the coast of Virginia and Maryland. There are two herds kept divided by a fence across the middle of the island, one herd belonging to Chincoteague Volunteer Fire Department, the other to Maryland. Living wild for hundreds of years, harsh conditions, and a diet of saltmarsh cordgrass and American beachgrass, plus a few other plants that grow on the island, have bred the horses down to a large pony size, between ten and fourteen hands. And, due to the high concentration of salt in their diet, not only do they have to drink more fresh water than domestic horses, but because of it, have a "fat" or "bloated" appearance. The herds are kept down by Maryland's use of birth control, while young colts from the Virginia herd are sold off once a year, at the end of July.

The name "Assateague" derives from an American Indian word that translates roughly to "land across the water." Assateague Island consists of three main areas: Assateague Island National Seashore, managed by the National Park Service; Assateague State Park, managed by Maryland's Department of Natural Resources; and Chincoteague National Wildlife Refuge, managed by the US Fish and Wildlife Service.

The Assateague ponies on the Maryland side are left on their own devices, though the National Park Service keeps their numbers to the required number of 150 by use of a contraceptive vaccine administered by a dart gun. But the Virginia herd is owned by Chincoteague Volunteer Fire Department. Each year on the last Wednesday and Thursday of July, the fire department's "saltwater cowboys" round up the ponies and herd them from the island to the mainland for the Pony Penning. The ponies are corralled and auctioned off on Thursday to those who want to buy one. The pony auction and the carnival held by the fire department earn revenue for them, since they would normally subsist on donations.

My husband and I, along with our friends, Deborah Painter, David Hawk, and Richard Hedges, went to Chincoteague and Assateague on July 26th. We missed this penning as it wasn't to happen until a few days later, but I know that my husband and I have plans to return next year to check it out. I was able to enjoy how much Chincoteague has embraced the ponies and especially Misty. I got to see the hoof prints left by Misty in the sidewalk in front of the Roxy Movie Theater. Across the street there's a statue of Misty.

A part of Assateague Island, where just beyond is the Atlantic Ocean.

In another part of Chincoteague is the Pony Centre, where not only was there much information about Misty, but I was also able to see a couple of wall murals discussing the pony legend. Also included were mentions of pirate legends—especially one particular pirate, Blackbeard. Outside of the centre is the grave of a granddaughter of Misty, along with ponies in corrals.

You can find out more abut this lovely centre at http://www.chincoteague.com/ponycentre/. It was there I heard that when she died, Misty was stuffed and can be seen. I didn't, as I couldn't handle that, same as years ago as a child I wouldn't let my parents take me to the Roy Rogers/Dale Evans Museum to see a stuffed Trigger. I did get to see the farm of the Beebees, the people who had bought Misty.

We drove across to Assateague and saw five of the ponies already corralled, waiting for the rest of the herd that the saltwater cowboys would soon be driving into the corral. Standing there among the crowds of tourists, I could imagine all the legends happening as I stared out at the sea. In my mind's eye, I saw Blackbeard or other pirates as they came to the island in a boat, maybe to escape their pursuers for a while, maybe even to bury their treasure. Another legend I imagined involved the ponies themselves.

The pony legend says that the horses swam to the island from a shipwrecked Spanish galleon. There is even mentioned on NationalGeographic.com that pirates brought the ponies to the island. A more plausible explanation is that they are the descendents of horses brought to the island in the seventeenth century by mainland owners who wanted to avoid the fencing laws and taxation of their livestock.

Even though the more logical tale is most likely the true one, I still opt for the more romantic one, for such a story adds mystique to these animals. Next time you want to see a wild horse, head to Assateague Island and let the sea breeze whisper in your ear their wonderful legend.

Mural of the legends of Assateague on a wall in the Chincoteague Pony Centre.

Chapter Twenty-Seven
Big Cats

Over the years, there are reports of big cats seen, those like lions, tigers, and panthers. Then like a specter, they vanish. Virginia, too, has its own stories of big cats.

Black Panther Mystery—Covington

There are stories that, back in the 1960s, a woman was riding her horse when suddenly, a black panther appeared. It startled her horse; it reared and threw its rider off. The woman screamed until she hit her head on a jagged piece of rock. They claim that some nights you can hear her still screaming along with the panther's bone-chilling cries. The rain on the rock will turn red where the big cat killed her, and then everything goes quiet.

Mountain Lions in Virginia?

Mountain Lions, also known as panther, painter, cougar, catamount, and snarlygoster, haven't been seen in Virginia since the nineteen hundreds. And yet, sightings of them have been reported since 1970, at least 121. This came from the Virginia Department of Game and Inland Fisheries.

In other states, there have been reports of mysterious animals seen—like African lions, tigers, and kangaroos. Why not Virginia? Especially an animal that existed in the state at one time.

Experts at Department of Game say they doubt there are mountain lions in Virginia, unless someone had one for a pet illegally and then released it. Is that what is happening here? Could some even have been escapees from a small zoo that is afraid to report that their animal (or animals) is loose? Are they the remnants of cougars that survived and live in the mountains, escaping industrialization of cities that are encroaching more and more upon the wilderness? Or is this another call for a cryptozoological creature that is nothing more than a myth?

Strange as it may seem, many of the sightings have been around the Fairfax area—not a wilderness by any stretch of the imagination. Of course, with garbage cans and small pets there, this would be a great source of easy-to-get food.

In early seventies, George Correll saw one of these big cats, followed by more sightings, which then halted. But in 1998, more cougars were observed and reported to the Virginia Game Department. One of these happened to one gentleman as he was retrieving his little dog that had wandered onto a neighbor's land. He stood about ten feet away from the cougar, shocked. Neither moved, just stared at each other. It was the tenth such report that Fairfax County wildlife expert Earl Hodnett had received that May

In 2004, the Staunton newspaper, *News Leader*, had an article of Joe Rowland who found a mountain lion on his property on July 19th. The man had pulled into his driveway, scanning his yard for wildlife as he always did. Usually he'd only see rabbits or deer, and when he noticed the tanned fur he assumed it belonged to a deer. As he drew nearer, he discovered that it was a cougar.

He rushed indoors to grab a digital camera to take a picture. He only got within sixty feet of the animal when it raised its head and stared at him. It bounded three leaps into the cornfield and Rowland stepped back. He held his camera high above his head and snapped the picture, then ran indoors. Joe printed the picture up for a friend, Roy Thompson, who checks game at IGA.

He took it into town and both stared at blow ups of the animal. Too big to be a bobcat and too cat-like for a small bear, they wondered if it was a mountain lion.

The article mentioned another sighting by a man as he drove his car through Showker Flats. When he saw the big cat, he slowed down to get a better view of it. He was pretty sure what he saw was a cougar.

But wildlife biologist, Al Bourgueouis, of Virginia Game Department doubted that they saw a cougar or even an African lion. Taking the height of the grass and more into account from the picture, it looked to be a smaller animal.

At the Web site, Cougar Quest, there have been sightings of cougars in places like Winchester and Alexandria, back in 2006. All are credible but unproven, though there had been one photo of what looked like a young puma taken in the summer of 2006, near Crozet, that had excited researchers.

But as posted on Cougar Quest, there hasn't been enough "hard evidence" to prove beyond all doubt that mountain lions are roaming the Northern Shenandoah Valley and elsewhere in the East. Though Virginia and West Virginia laws do list this species as endangered, they don't believe it exists in the wild in these states. Yet Cougar Quest does take seriously any reported sightings of these big cats in Virginia and works hard to prove that this endangered species exists and needs to be protected. So if anyone lives in the areas stated on the Web site and has seen a mountain lion, you can report the sighting at http://www.btcent.com/CougarQuest.htm.

Note: Since I wrote this chapter, a cougar or female African lion has been reported in the south Richmond area. I caught the report on the local news, November 12, 2008. This particular sighting happened in the 1400 block of Brownleaf Drive in Richmond—the Bramblewood Estates Apartments. The woman who spotted the big cat told her neighbors that when she went outside, a mountain lion chased her. She was able to jump in her car and get away before it got to her. Once called, the animal control officers searched the apartment complex but didn't find any sign of the big cat. Concerned, the neighbors knew this location was not too far from Bon Air, where there have been sightings of a mountain lion or even what they thought of as a female African lion for the better part of a month.

Next time you go backpacking in the wilds of the Shenandoah Valley, or go for a walk in Bon Air and see something suspicious that looks like a cougar, it just might be.

Chapter Twenty-Eight
Devil Monkeys—Saltville

Devil Monkeys are described as baboon-like creatures able to leap like kangaroos. They have dark, "mean" eyes, pointed ears, short to shaggy fur that varies from red to gray to black, and large flat feet. It is said that these creatures won't back down, even from dogs, and although they are thought to be vegetarians, there are tales of them killing livestock and small game. They exhibit a range of primate hoots, calls, screeches, whistles, and unearthly screams. Worse, they have an odor so bad that they have been also called Skunk Apes.

A cryptozoologist, Chad Arment, investigated sightings of these creatures that one Virginia family and their friends had experiences with. This occurred from 1959-1990s, in the mountains that surround Saltville.

Paranormal investigators Pauline and James Boyd's parents were attacked in 1959 by a creature that left three scratch marks on their car. Not long after, a couple of nurses were driving home when an unknown animal attacked their vehicle, ripping the convertible's top off. Badly shaken, they escaped otherwise unharmed.

Friends of Pauline saw one of these creatures trotting across the road in front of their car. It leaped over a ditch, glided over a fence, and leaped through weeds along the road.

What are these devil monkeys? An illusion caused from being too tired from driving, a baboon, or some animal unknown to man? Maybe even a sort of Sasquatch? Whatever they are, devil monkeys are just another mystery animal unique to Virginia.

Chapter Twenty-Nine
Virginian Urban Legends

The definition of urban legend is an apocryphal, secondhand story told as true and plausible enough to be believed. It is likely to be framed as a cautionary tale, about some horrible, embarrassing, ironic, or exasperating series of events that supposedly happened to a real person. It is also known as an urban myth, urban belief tale, contemporary legend or migratory legend—stories like the one of the dotty grandmother who tried to dry her wet poodle in the microwave and it exploded, or the man with the hatchet on lover's lane. Strange as it may seem, though most of these turn out to be false, there are those very few that have a basis in truth—like the Richmond vampire. Some may actually start with a basis in truth, but over the years have been spread to other places, making what may be truth in one spot, not so in others.

Common characteristics of an urban legend are: It is usually a narrative, alleged to be true, plausible enough to be believed, its veracity is unproven, it is of spontaneous origin, it varies in the telling, it takes the form of a tale of caution, is attributed to trustworthy secondhand sources, and is transmitted from individual to individual, either in oral or written form (fax, photocopy or email).

If such a tale is sent to you in your email or someone told you verbally a story that you aren't sure is true, look it up on snopes.com. Or you can pick up some great books filled with urban legends. Here is a link where you can check out the names of some of those books: http://urbanlegends.about.com/library/weekly/aatpulbooks.htm.

One urban legend is the Richmond vampire. The werewolf of Henrico is another. There's even the Bunnyman. With cities growing bigger and more populated, the kind of tale your grandfather told you back on the farm has taken on a more urban setting.

No Dogs or Sailors on the Grass!—Norfolk

An urban legend still believed today in Norfolk, Virginia, is one that author Deborah Painter, who also happens to live in the city, reported to me. It concerns the story that there are signs posted in the city, saying that both sailors and dogs are to keep off the grass.

Sometimes men and women of the Navy may not feel as welcome by civilian residents of the city. Some locals are said to view sailors, soldiers, and Air Force personnel on leave as marauding hordes, out to get drunk, start fights, wreck property, and despoil the womenfolk. As posted on Snopes.com by historian George Holbert Tucker, he never saw any such sign in the city's local lore.

The most common encounters of this rumor persisted in the 1940s, though there had been earlier reports in the Tidewater area of Virginia in the 1930s. I myself was told by someone, in a writers' group I am a member of, that his father had been stationed in Norfolk during World War II and saw those very signs. I mentioned that Snopes.com had investigated it and found that the signs never existed. So, is the research of Snopes incomplete, or has the writer's father been a victim of an urban legend spread by another serviceman at the time?

The next sightings took place in the sixties. There were claims that the Navy told the city to take them down and were told no. Strangely enough, this story began to travel around and there were those who "saw" these signs in Jacksonville, Florida, and in Portsmouth, Maine, around 1970. There were also some sightings from the west coast in the 1940s—for instance, in San Diego, California.

If these tales aren't real, where did they come from? They may well have sprung from the tales of a seaman who traversed the seas about a century before sailors began swearing to one another that they'd run into these signs in the United States. In *Before the Wind*, the memoirs set down by Captain Charles Tyng, there is an account of a sign encountered at Cowes on the Isle of Wight—a small island to the south of England. He had gone ashore to enjoy the land after being at sea so long and became disgusted when he found a

Downtown Norfolk, Virginia.

sign reading, "Dogs and sailors are forbidden to trespass here." His twenty-five years at sea would have enabled him to come to Norfolk many times, and one can see how he would tell this yarn to various sailors, along with spreading it to his own shipmates. In turn, like all stories told orally, in time the city's name became Norfolk and not Cowes as the place that really displayed these signs.

The Washing Machine Story—Charlottesville

There is an urban legend of a thirty-nine-year-old Charlottesville man who died in a freak accident that involved his washing machine. According to police reports, Samuel Randolph Strickson was doing laundry when he tried to speed up the process. Strickson apparently tried to stuff approximately fifty pounds of laundry into his washing machine by climbing on top of the washer and attempting to force the clothing into the basin. It was then that he kicked the washing machine's ON button. When the machine turned on, the man lost his balance and both of his feet went into the machine, getting stuck.

The machine started its cycle and, frantic, Strickson tried to free himself by thrashing around. He banged his head against a nearby shelf and knocked over a bottle of bleach. The bleach apparently opened or the cap came off. It poured over his face, blinding him, and he even swallowed some of it. He threw up just as his dog came into the laundry room. At that same time, a large box of baking soda fell off the same shelf the bleach had been on and startled the dog, which then urinated. By the police reports, it seems that urine, like vinegar, is acidic, and the chemical reaction between that and the baking soda resulted in a small explosion. The dog escaped unharmed. The washing machine with Strickson still stuck in it went into its high-speed spin cycle, spinning him around at seventy miles per hour, at least by the forensic reports. Stickson's head slammed into a steel beam behind the machine, killing him. A neighbor heard the commotion and dialed 911, but when the police got there he was pronounced dead at the scene.

Is this true? Not a word. Seems this one is being sent around in an email in the Darwin Awards ("Honoring those who improve the species...by accidentally removing themselves from it...")

Magic of Love at U of R—Richmond

Supposedly, there's an urban legend of a magical spot on the campus of the University of Richmond. Legend has it that if two people kiss under the gazebo near the lake, which is in the center of campus, they will eventually marry. The only way to break the charm (or curse, depending on your views on commitment) is to jump into the lake. Several students have kissed at the gazebo and wondered if their fates have been forever changed. Incidentally, it is said that quite a few have also jumped into the lake to save their souls from marriage.

The gazebo near the lake on the campus of University of Richmond.

Urban Legend of
J. J. Kelly High School—Wise

There is this myth that tells of a student at J. J. Kelly High School who hung himself in the auditorium. Before he did so, it was said that he rode the elevator up to the second floor, walked down the long hallway, and got a drink of water from a water fountain. To this day the elevator opens and closes.

The funny thing is, the elevator wasn't put in until 1995, and this story happened before that. Another urban legend laid to rest.

The Civil War Statues—Richmond

Another interesting local lore that has been proven as false on Snopes.com states that the statues of General Stonewall Jackson, Robert E. Lee, J.E.B. Stuart, and Confederate President Jefferson Davis are pointed in well-defined directions that symbolized if they

Statue of Robert E. Lee riding Traveller in Richmond.

Statue of JEB Stuart on his horse in Richmond.

died or survived the Civil War. Facing north meant they died, south, they lived. Except when one studies the statues' directions, one finds that indeed Lee faces south and lived, while Jackson faces north and died. Stuart's horse faces north and was mortally wounded at Yellow Tavern in 1864. But Stuart and Davis are looking toward the east, so what can that mean?

Byrd Theatre Does Not Have a Swimming Pool—Richmond

There are stories online about the restrooms at the Byrd Theatre in Carytown, saying that they are haunted like other areas in the place. The truth is that the ghost, Robert Coulter, doesn't haunt them. This is just one of many myths about the theater. As he told me when interviewed about the haunting there for my book, *Haunted Richmond, Virginia*, the current manager, Todd Schall-Vess believes that people have gotten the haunted restrooms tale confused with one from another theatre in Richmond, the Landmark. It happens

Byrd Theatre in Carytown.

all the time, and not just with the haunted restrooms, either. People come to the theater and ask about the swimming pool, mistaking the underground spring beneath Byrd for one. Of course, there is a theater in Richmond that does have a swimming pool, but it's not the Byrd. That too is the Landmark, whose swimming pool measures twenty by seventy foot.

The Odor Under the Bed—Alexandria

An urban legend that circulates across the United States may have its origins in a real Virginia event. Found online at Snopes. com and at http://www.halloweenghoststories.com/, the story tells of a couple who checked into a remote hotel and got a whiff of a rotting odor that came from the bed. Upset, they alerted the desk clerk. The clerk checked the bed out and discovered a dead body in the box springs.

Most people would not believe this tale. But in 1989, a murderer actually used this method to get rid of his two victims. The first one, a twenty-seven-year-old woman was discovered under the floor of a motel room on Route 1 in Alexandria. The second, a twenty-nine-year-old woman was found beneath a bed in another Alexandria motel. Apparently in the first case, the murderer partially hid the body under the bed and then put it under the floorboards. He didn't move out of either room for several weeks.

Hitchhiker on Walney Road—Chantilly

There is the persistent urban legend of the hitchhiker anywhere you go. Most of the time, it is a young woman who is killed on her way home from a party. On the anniversary of her death, she catches a ride only to vanish when the drivers reaches the address given.

But another kind of hitchhiker is seen on Walney Road, at one of three locations. The story goes that if he is not picked up for the third time the driver catches sight of him, he will appear in the passenger seat and force the driver off the road. There are those who say the number of accidents on the road is caused by this nasty ghost.

The story behind this is that one evening a man was walking along the road when he was struck and killed by a passing vehicle. The hit and run driver had never been found. It is said that the spirit is searching for the car that hit him.

Haunted Junkyard—Bassett

There is an urban legend about a junkyard in Bassett. It seems that there are those who say they have seen headlights of the abandoned cars flashing on and off. Plus they have heard sounds of car doors opening and shutting, along with car radios playing. There are even sounds of vehicle engines racing and cars driving back and forth.

Are these the spirits of those killed in car wrecks, as the crumpled machines end up here? Or just another urban legend?

The Mythical Lost City—Richmond

There's an urban legend in Richmond that a lost city is located off Portugee Road. Supposedly, the city is in the woods somewhere near the Richmond International Airport. All kinds of stories about it involve government agents, Satanists, Bigfoot, cannibalistic madmen that are offspring of former asylum inmates, and even something called the Stickman. But there is no proof that there exists such a city.

Note: Such a place exists—as I saw on the news in November 2008. Though I can not track down the report mentioned on the local news, I found some basic information on it.

It looks like an average sub-division of the late fifties, with paved streets and fire hydrants on every block, sidewalks and street lights, even a working sewer system that carried summer run-off to parts unknown.

There were plenty of theories as to the origin of this urban ghost town. Aliens from space, a fake "city" to decoy Japanese bomber pilots from the nearby airport and Richmond City, an ill-conceived housing development that went bust, causing it's patron to hang himself from one of his own street lights.

During World War II, Virginia became one of the most prosperous states in America. The ship yards in Norfolk provided the war ships and a very busy port for combat soldiers. The numerous military bases in Virginia made it a hub for military operations. Richmond, at the time, played a very important role. The Richmond airport, then named the Byrd Airport, served as a landing for many military operations.

Money was appropriated, and a second, fake Richmond was built outside of the city. In the event of an air raid, power to the real Richmond would be cut and lights would go on in the fake city. Apparently from the air it looked similar enough to the Richmond of that time, that from the sky the enemy wouldn't be able to tell the difference.

The weirdest thing, there are claims that the beginnings of a national urban myth was born because of this "Lost City"—that there was an insane asylum called the old Charenton Plantation just down the road from it. The story goes that an inmate escaped from the asylum. Thrashing his way through the thick forest surrounding Lost City, he burst from the brush and frightened a couple of kids who were making out in the back seat of a '57 Chevy.

The terrified kids saw a scimitar he happened to be carrying and thought it was a hook where his right hand should have been. And that is, supposedly, where the man with the hook urban legend was born. But except for one place, I can't prove if this is where this myth started or not.

To visit the Lost City, take the 64 E to the Laburnum exit, bear right and then take a left on Williamsburg. Pass the airport, then through Sandston, and when you come to a light, turn right onto Technology Boulevard. The entrance to the Lost City is off the boulevard.

The Bunnyman Bridge in Clifton—a blue orb is captured in the photo also.

Chapter Thirty
The Bunnyman—Clifton

There are urban legends of the killer with the hook or the murderer loose on Lover's Lane, but Virginia (and some parts of Maryland) has its own urban legend: the Bunnyman.

Any story involving a figure dressed in a white bunny suit armed with an ax, threatening children or vandalizing property is memorable. When the details get juicy—mutilated animals, murdered children, bodies hanging from bridges—well, you have a unique urban legend.

The legend is set around a concrete tunnel of a Southern Railway overpass on Colchester Road in Clifton, Virginia, nicknamed the "Bunnyman Bridge." This place is set not far from the intersection of Fairfax Station Road and Colchester Road, right on Colchester Road. After my first failed attempt to get a picture of it by finding a Colchester Road that was a dead-end with homes being built along it, I found out in another book, *Ghost Hunting in Virginia* by Michael J. Varhola, where it really was.

On Sunday, November 16, 2008, my husband drove us there so I could finally see the infamous place for myself and get a picture. When we drove right up to it, Bill parked the car and I got out and walked up to take some pictures of it. A strange itchy feeling came over me, like someone was watching me. I took the pictures. It was then I noticed in the camera viewfinder that I had captured a bright blue orb in three of the photos! Actually, the orb began to form itself in the first one and was a teardrop shape in the second. [Note: I found a fourth picture, where the blue orb was starting to develop, with a shiny white one in the green leaves that the place was covered in. That white orb had vanished by the next picture.]

I ran back to the car, gave Bill the camera, and grabbed my electronic voice recorder to try and record, hopefully, something in audio on it. I only did this for a minute, for though no vehicle had come up the road either way, it didn't mean sooner or later one wouldn't. Strangest thing when I asked if anyone was there, a sudden gust of wind swept into the tunnel, spinning leaves against the walls. After that, no wind at all. Who knows? Something felt weird about that tunnel. Maybe not the Bunnyman, but something, that was for sure.

The story of the Bunnyman, which circulated in Northern Virginia and Maryland since the seventies, had been featured in high school newspapers and on the Internet, kept mostly alive by teens and college students. It is said that if you go to the bridge on Halloween, the Bunnyman's ghost will appear and kill you at midnight. Teenagers go in groups, or a few, to party as they wait, hoping to catch a glimpse of him.

Bunnyman's fame doesn't stop there. This unusual ax-wielding killer dressed in a bunny costume became the subject of a segment on *Scariest Places on Earth* on the Fox Channel. The segment, "Terror on Bunnyman's Bridge," broadcasted in 2001. The Bunnyman went from local legend to national, maybe even worldwide, status, alongside the legends of Bloody Mary and the hatchet murderers of Lover's Lane.

There are even films on him on YouTube. One is the Legend of the Bunnyman, a short film at http://www.youtube.com/watch?v=z5Bk4CXebP0. And there's also the Bunny Man Documentary at http://www.youtube.com/watch?v=D-54cB-Ie6s&NR=1. These and many more at YouTube reveal that the spooky tales of the Bunnyman are alive and well.

There's also a horror movie that's a cult film: *Donnie Darko*. Did the Bunnyman legend inspire this film? There are claims that it did. The movie takes place in the town of Middlesex, Virginia, and features Frank, an ominous character, dressed in a bunny suit. If you've never seen this movie, you can rent it at a video store or purchase it at Amazon.com, or various other places where DVDs are for sale. Could be a good way to spend the evening!

The Urban Legend

The myth first popped up in 1976. The first story has the Bunnyman responsible for the deaths of two children in Clifton. Rumors of the disappearance of other children, plus the horrible mutilations of animals, circulated during the telling of the story that year. No one dared go out at night, at least not near the bridge where this psycho was said to be seen hanging around.

In 1992, more had been added to the legend, this time telling of murdered children hung from a covered bridge, the supposed killer, an inmate escapee dressed in a bunny suit. The Bunnyman earned his nickname because he nourished himself on rabbits while pursued by the police; other variations of the tale had him hunting rabbits and using their pelts to make clothing for himself.

Years later, when people began using the Internet, this terrifying legend was reborn. Like all urban legends, it rose to new heights. One widely circulated version on the Net has inmates from an insane asylum escaping in 1904 while being transferred to Lorton prison. One of the inmates was named Douglas J. Grifon. He murdered fellow inmate Marcus Wallster and then became the Bunnyman. The location, plus the names of several victims Grifon killed as the Bunnyman and dates of their murders are mentioned. It even adds that anyone could check the Clifton Town Library to verify these facts.

Of course, it's been proven false. There has never been an insane asylum in Fairfax County. Lorton Prison never came to be until 1910. And when it did, it was part of the District of Columbia corrections system, not Virginia's. Adding to the falsifications, neither Wallster nor Grifon appeared in any court records. Pounding the final nail into this story, no Clifton Town Library exists, either. Is it possible that this story is a fictional account with the makings of a great horror story? Could be. . .

Another Web site, Urban Legends and Superstitions at http://urbanlegendsonline.com/bridgestracks/bunnyman.html posted the same story, adding that a note was left on the inmate, Marcus, who supposedly was found hanging from the tunnel entrance beneath Bunnyman Bridge; the words on that piece of paper said: "You'll never find me, no matter how hard you try! Signed, The Bunnyman." The Web site goes on to say that if you walk all the way down the tunnel at around midnight, the Bunnyman will grab you and hang you from the entrance of the bridge. There's a story set in 2001 was also posted telling of a guide and six local students (no mention if they were in high school or college) had found mutilated rabbit parts, heard noises, and thought they saw figures moving in the woods. Frightened, they left the area.

There are many stories told by young people about Bunnyman. I mentioned a couple of sites on the Web with some stories, but there are others on the Internet, a great breeding ground for the Bunnyman legend.

Enjoy some of the variations of the Bunnyman legend that I discovered. These are the more up-to-date ones, showing that Bunnyman is alive and well, and still scaring people.

In Reston, Virginia, there used to be a dirt road leading off Sunset Hills Road, just before it intersected with Reston Avenue. The kids in town knew that it led to the Bunnyman's house. Supposedly, one Halloween night he dressed up in a bunny costume, shot his wife and kids, then opened the door to trick-or-treaters all night with the corpses of his family still in the house.

Another tale had a guy in a bunny costume standing in the middle of the road at the bottom of a hill in Clifton. As cars came down the hill, he would throw an ax at the vehicle and somehow, he always killed the person or persons inside.

There's the tale of a mental patient that escaped from a bus transporting patients when it crashed in the woods near the bridge. The authorities were called in, but when they searched for the man, they never found him. Later, carcasses of rabbits began to be found, scattered around the bridge. It seems that the mental patient was living in the woods, surviving off of the meat of the rabbits. But when they discovered some teenagers gutted and hanging from the bridge, the local authorities put out a manhunt for "the Bunnyman," as the local children called him. The story goes that they eventually caught up with him. Just as they were about to apprehend the Bunnyman, though, he jumped in front of a train roaring down the tracks. Since then, it is said that the Bunnyman's spirit haunts the bridge, and that on Halloween, at midnight, his spirit becomes visible right over the bridge that bears his name. Drunken teenagers can always be found at the base of the bridge at midnight on Halloween, waiting to see if the spirit of Bunnyman will appear.

Another take on the legend has a young man from Clifton, Virginia who came upon the bridge while traveling. Later, he killed his parents and dragged their bodies into the woods to hang them from the bridge, and then committed suicide. In 1943, three teenagers, two men and a young woman, went to the Bunnyman Bridge on Halloween night. The next morning they were found dead, hung from the bridge, their bodies slashed open. Notes were found attached to their feet, with the words written on them," You'll never catch the Bunnyman!"

One witness had his own personal experiences with Bunnyman Bridge. He has been out there about a dozen times, since it's about fifteen minutes from his house. Most of the time, he and his friends would hang out there, waiting to see if anything would happen. Nothing happened, but they got this feeling that someone or something was watching them. Even though the bridge is located about twenty-five miles from Washington D.C., it is still in the middle of nowhere. Only a few houses nestle within the woods that surround the bridge and railroad tracks.

The last time he and his buddies went out there, they heard voices that came from the woods, whispers that sounded as if they originated twenty feet from where the young men stood. Frightened, they bolted.

Was Bunnyman ever real? Many legends may begin with a kernel of truth somewhere in their murky pasts. Brian A. Conley, a historian-archivist at the Fairfax County Public Library, haunted by this "rascally rabbit," pursued extensive research if see if there had ever really been a real Bunnyman.

Possible Truth

Brian Conley found 550 individual mentions of killings in Fairfax County from 1872 through 1973. Eliminating most of domestic murders and concentrating on multiple murders, especially those involving children, he got it down to three with possibilities.

Case One

One case involved the gruesome murders of Frances and her eight-month-old daughter, June Holober, in February 1949. The convicted killer was Frances's husband and June's father, Charles Holober. Though Charles was sentenced to die in the electric chair, his attorney filed an appeal alleging that the jury failed to give proper consideration to the plea of insanity. The Virginia Supreme Court of Appeals overturned the conviction and ordered a new trial and Holober was re-committed to the Western State Mental Hospital at Marion, Virginia. While there, he was judged insane.

Case Two

The second case involved Minnie, Loretta, and Catherine Ridgeway in March 1927. The senseless murders of the children, Loretta and Catherine, shocked the community of Fairfax. Louis Boersig called at the Ridgeway home, looking for Mr. Ridgeway, and was told he was not at home. Louis attacked Minnie, knocked her unconscious and bludgeoned the girls. He stole money and bolted. A neighbor found them and all three were taken to Alexandria Hospital. Loretta died on arrival, Catherine eight days later, but the mother survived to identify the assailant. The police arrested Louis at his home and three months later, he was convicted.

Case Three

The last case happened in August 1918, and involved Eva Roy, the fourteen-year-old daughter of Danish immigrant Peter Roy. One morning, she went out to tend her father's herd of cows. When she didn't come home that night, her father organized a search, and twenty-four hours later, they discovered her body tied to a tree in the woods near the old Hanse House.

There were several suspects. One was William Wooster, age sixteen, recently released from an insane asylum, but evidence found that he had been nowhere near the scene of Eva's murder.

The next one was a soldier who deserted from Camp A. A. Humphries (now Fort Belvoir). The soldier was located some days later near Charlottesville, Virginia, his face and hands scratched and wearing freshly laundered clothes. He claimed to have no memory of the events between leaving Camp Humphries and his capture. After weeks of investigation, the police determined that he had not committed the crime.

Then the police apprehended Ben Ruben, an escaped inmate from Lorton Prison. Ruben had been serving a three-year sentence for breaking and entering, and admitted to killing Eva. An investigator sent by the Commonwealth of Virginia concluded that he was not responsible for the crime. Ruben changed his plea and then denied killing Eva, and was not able to locate the area of the attack. Two days later, he escaped from the Fairfax jail and when he tried to buy a pistol, he admitted that he concocted his story in order to be transferred to Fairfax, because escape would be easier from there.

The last person arrested, Lou Hall, was tried for the murder in Fairfax County Court, but his first trial resulted in a hung jury. Nine votes said guilty, three, innocent. A second trial resulted in a not guilty for him. After that, no one else was arrested and Eva's murderer has never been found.

The Reality?

It appeared that none of these three murders had been committed by the Bunnyman. Bunnyman murders were always spectacular and the body count pretty high, as in the version with thirty-two victims, mostly children, as told on the Web site, Castle of Spirits. There were two reports by University of Maryland student Patricia Johnson in a paper titled, "The Bunnyman." She turned it in as part of coursework for a class entitled "Introduction to Folklore," focusing on the Bunnyman. The interviewees were students ranging in age from fifteen to eighteen. The reason she did this was because the tale met all of the qualifications for an urban legend. It was set in an urban setting, existed prior to her project, and had appeared in print as truth. Of the fifty-four variations though, only two incidents that happened in the 1970s might explain the reality of the Bunnyman.

I could only find two incidents *anywhere* that might be what she had. The first incident happened on the evening of October 20, 1970. United States Air Force Academy cadet Bob Bennett and his fiancée, Dusty, had returned from football game around midnight. They parked the car in a field on Guinea Road, so they could talk. They noticed something moving outside the rear window. Moments later, the front passenger window shattered and they saw a white-clad figure standing near the broken window. Bennett turned the engine on and he then turned the car around. The man screamed at them. "You're on private property and I have your tag number."

Driving away, they discovered a hatchet on the car floor. When the police asked for a description of the man, Bob insisted he wore a white suit with long bunny ears. All Dusty could remember was something white and pointed, like a Ku Klux Klan outfit. Both remembered the man's face, though, but in the darkness they weren't so sure about his race. The police returned the hatchet to Bennett after examination. Bennett was required to report the incident upon his return to his base.

The second reported sighting occurred the evening of October 29, 1970. Construction security guard Paul Phillips approached a strangely-dressed man he found standing on the porch of an unfinished home in Kings Park West on Guinea Road. The man looked about twenty years old and wore a gray, black, and white bunny suit. He began to chop at a porch post with a long-handled axe and said to Phillips, "All you people trespass around here. If you don't get out of here, I'm going to bust you on the head." Then he took off into the woods.

Now Mr. Conley went and checked police reports about these two incidents himself. There was no official record of the assault on Robert Bennett and his fiancé. There was an investigation report in relation to the October 29th incident though. Police had responded to a call about a "a subject dressed as a rabbit with an ax" vandalizing property at 5307 Guinea Road. They never found the "bunny man." They turned the case over to an investigator of the Criminal Investigation Bureau, who visited the construction offices of the Kings Park West Subdivision, but found nothing. He did receive a phone call after he left, that someone called the "Axe Man" phoned the construction company. The construction company thought the voice sounded young, as if the caller was in his early twenties. The police staked out the place that night, but nothing came of it. Had this been a Halloween prank on the construction company?

In November, the police received a call from a woman that her son knew the identity of the Bunnyman, but interviewing him and other children in the area got them nothing at all. Unable to solve the case; it was marked as inactive.

There have even been paranormal investigators at the tunnel. One such group from Maryland had sensed something there when they went to investigate it. They felt the place had a lot of negative energy associated with it and that it may even be haunted, though the cause for the haunting is still undetermined. There have been stories of many deaths there over the years; whether or not these deaths really happened, and whether the presence they encountered is related to the Bunnyman was a question that they couldn't answer.

The next time you decide to check out Bunnyman's Bridge, especially on Halloween night, watch out for rabbits. Especially if one of those bunnies looks bigger than normal, and after standing up, and suddenly is clutching an axe. RUN!

Chapter Thirty-One
Witches in Virginia

Double, double, toil and trouble
Fire burn, and cauldron bubble...

~William Shakespeare.

Witchcraft, in various historical, anthropological, religious, and mythological contexts, includes the use of certain kinds of supernatural or magical powers. A witch is a practitioner of witchcraft. While mythological witches are often supernatural creatures, historically, many people have been accused of witchcraft, or have claimed to be witches. Witches have stereotypically, though not exclusively, been women. There have been men, too. If the woman was older, lived alone with maybe only a cat for company, and had extensive knowledge of herbs, then a jealous neighbor could use this to accuse her of witchcraft. Especially if the accused had a nice piece of property the neighbor wanted. Or fought off sexual advances from the neighbor.

Witches are as much a part of Virginia's history and folklore as anywhere else. There were homes in Virginia that have witch doors—crosses carved on the paneled doors to keep the witches away—and people made witch bottles to protect them against witches, though the bottles were used mainly in the Tidewater area. There is even a rumor of a witch who emits a green light when seen flying through the trees in the Old House Woods in Mathews. There is no mention if the witch is female or male. In Stafford, there is a trail off Telegraph Road that leads to a place called Witches Pond. There is supposed to be a sacrifice table there used in the 1700s with letters in Latin carved on it. Numerous sightings of a woman have been seen near it. I found online that there was a witch's creek behind where Aquia Harbor is now. Supposedly, this is why the place is haunted.

Then of course, Virginia has its famous or infamous witches—like the Witch of Pungo, Grace Sherwood.

Due to the fame of the Witch of Pungo, there are businesses and a road named after her.

Protections Against Witches Used in Virginia

There were many ways Virginians protected themselves against witches. The first three methods were a mixture of Celtic and African American lore.

1. Leave a bowl of salt outside your door. It is said that witches love to count the grains. A witch will sit down and count each grain. By the time she/he finishes, it will be morning and you will be safe. (Ditto with a broom, for the witch will count the broom straws.) Strangely enough, this is in myths about vampires too.

2. Hang a used horseshoe above your door. Before a witch enters the house, she must go down every road the horse has traveled when he wore that shoe. By the time she finishes, the dawn will be on its way, and you'll be safe.

3. Witches hate the color blue because it is the color of heaven. African Americans, especially in South Carolina and Georgia, painted the trim of their homes blue for protection.

Witch Bottles

A common counterspell against illness caused by witchcraft was to put the sick person's urine in a bottle with iron nails, brass pins, and pieces of lead, cork it tightly, and either set it to heat by the hearth or bury it in the ground. Joseph Blagrave wrote in 1671 that a witch's bottle, "will endanger the witches' life, for ... they will be grievously tormented, making their water with great difficulty, if any at all." The theory was that the witch created a magical link with her victim and this could be reversed, using the victim's body-products. The witch had to break the link to save herself. The victim would then recover.

The recipe was still known in a Norfolk village in 1939: Take a stone bottle, make water in it, and fill it with your own toe-nails and finger-nails, iron nails, and anything which belongs to you. Hang the bottle over the fire and keep stirring it. It must be dark in the room and you can't speak or make any noise. Then the witch is supposed to come to your door and beg you to open the door to let her in. If you keep silent and ignore her, the witch will burst. In the folklore,

This witch bottle belongs to author Deborah Painter.

it is said that the strain on the mind of the person when the witch begs to be let in is usually so great that the person breaks down and speaks. Then the witch is set free.

In London, England, seventeenth-century pottery jugs of the kind called "greybeards" or "bellarmines" were found buried in ditches or streams. They contained bent nails and felt hearts stuck with pins. In Essex and Suffolk, others had been discovered, underneath the hearths or thresholds of houses. Later, cheap glass bottles would be used in the same way. One was unearthed under the hearth of a Sussex cottage in the 1860s, as was common in the country. It contained two hundred bent pins. An example that dated from the early years of the twentieth century turned up in a shop at Padstow, Cornwall. Urine was put in a cod-liver-oil bottle which had its cork pierced with eight pins and one needle, and then bricked up in a chimney. In Cambridgeshire, a three-sided iron bottle held hen's blood and feathers mingled with the usual human urine, salt, hair, and nail-clippings; also (for protection rather than cure) small bottles of greenish or bluish glass filled with colored silk threads. These had been displayed beside doors or windows, to divert the witch's power by confusing her gaze. According to the *East London Advertiser* on August 1, 1903, a barber in Essex was asked to save some hair-clippings from a customer's neck. This was so someone who wanted revenge on the man could place them in a bottle and then heat it until at midnight it burst, making the man ill. Not a defensive counter spell, instead this was an active magic attack, using the intended victim's hair; sometimes, witch bottles were similarly used.

Belinda Nash of Ferry Plantation, an expert on Grace Sherwood, the "Witch of Pungo," told me that people put in human urine, a piece of lead, an iron nail, and a brass pin. They have a witch bottle on display at Ferry Plantation, so next time you're in Virginia Beach, take a tour of the house and go look at it.

Belinda also told me about "witch balls." It seems in Scotland, people used to wear them around their necks to ward off witches. It was also believed in Scotland and Canada that if a witch touched one, her/his soul would be caught within the ball forever.

A witch ball is a hollow sphere of plain or stained glass hung in cottage windows in eighteenth-century England to ward off evil spirits, witch's spells, or ill fortune, though the witch's ball actually originated among cultures where witches were considered a blessing. Witches would usually "enchant" the balls to enhance their potency against evils. Later, they were often posted on top of a vase or suspended by a cord (as from the mantelpiece or rafters) for a decorative effect. Witch balls appeared in America in the nineteenth century and were often found in gardens under the name "gazing ball," something that has come back, as I bought one last summer to place in my own garden. However, "gazing balls" contain no strands within their interior. According to folk tales, witch balls would entice evil spirits with their bright colors; the strands inside the ball would then capture the spirit and prevent it from escaping.

Witch balls sometimes measure as large as seven inches (eighteen cm) in diameter. By tradition, but not always, the witch ball is green or blue in color and made from glass. There have been others made of wood, grass, or twigs, instead of glass. Some are decorated in enameled swirls and brilliant stripes of various colors. The gazing balls found in many of today's gardens are derived from silvered witch balls that acted as convex mirrors, warding off evil by reflecting it away.

Because they look similar to the glass balls used on fishing nets, witch balls are often associated with sea superstitions and legends. The modern Christmas ornament ball is descended from the witch ball. According to an ancient tale, the ornament was originally placed on the tree to dispel a visitor's envy at the presents left beneath the tree.

Unlike the cases in Salem, Massachusetts, where women had been accused unjustly and declared guilty, then hung, Virginia seemed to handle the witchcraft thing much better. To curb runaway charges of witchcraft like in New England, the Virginia General Assembly passed in 1662, "An Act for Punishment of Scandalous Persons." It stated that women who acted peculiar and scandalous and caused their husbands to bring suits against those accusing their wives of witchcraft, after judgment had been passed, the woman would be punished by ducking. If the slander was enormous, the damages were adjusted at a greater amount then five hundred pounds of tobacco.

This made many think carefully before accusing someone of witchcraft or suing for slander if their wife or husband was accused of being a witch.

Witches Stories

In the second half of the seventeenth century, one detected a witch by finding a witch's mark on the accused. This was thought to be an extra "teat," generally below the left breast, though I don't doubt if found elsewhere the accusers didn't also take this as a sign. This teat enabled the Devil to suck his victims and collaborators.

There are documented cases of searches like this. One happened in Norfolk County in 1679, where charges brought against Mrs. Alice Cartwrite, said that she had "bewitched" her child and caused its death. The sheriff had a panel of women search her body for evidence of her being a witch. But they found nothing out of the ordinary and she was ordered acquitted.

Witches and devils have been in Virginia since the first colonists settled in Jamestown. In L. B. Taylor's *Ghosts of Virginia Volume VI*, he mentions King James saying how "devils" were considered to be in wild areas of the world, and that the Devil is present in places of greatest ignorance and barbarity. One can imagine what John Smith and the others thought when they saw the Native Americans with their dances, painted faces, and other tribal traditions. Of course, I would say that ignorance was more on the settlers' side than the Indians' in this.

Virginia was deemed a dwelling place of evil and a battleground between the forces of good and evil. Idols worshiped by Indians were considered representations of the Devil. One such idol, "Okee," was considered to be a "devil-witch" by John Smith himself. And when one of the colonists, Alexander Whitaker, and others with him, explored the Nansemond River, they came upon some Indians doing a dance. One of the natives told them that there would be rain shortly. When a storm struck, Whitaker wrote, "All which things make me think that there be great witches amongst them and they (are) very familiar with the devil."

Unlike Alice Cartwrite, other accused witches did not fare well. The first case of suspected witchcraft occurred in September 1626, when Goodwife Joan Wright of Surry County was charged with practicing the craft. A man, Giles Allingstone, claimed that she had put a spell on him. He said that, for twelve months, any game that he shot at, he could never kill. He also alleged that when Goody Wright had been dismissed as a midwife—due to her being left-handed—he, his wife, and their baby all suffered lingering illnesses.

It grew worse for the poor woman. A woman named Rebecca Graye testified that Goody Wright made a correct prophesy that Graye's husband and two other married men would soon be buried, which they were. When a man, Robert Thresher, was going to send two of his hens to Elizabeth Arundle, Goody Wright prophesized, that Elizabeth would be dead by the time the chickens got to her. This premonition was fulfilled, too. Another testimony had Goody Wright telling a woman who had stolen a stick of firewood from a fort that if she didn't return it, she would be made to dance stark naked. The testimony went on to say that the woman gave back the firewood the next day.

Though brought to trial, there is no evidence that Goody Wright had ever been convicted or punished.

In 1654, according to author and historian Richard Beale Davis, there was a conviction of witchcraft in Virginia that resulted in an execution on a ship bound for Jamestown. At that time, witches were believed to conjure up storms at sea, along with causing widespread illness among the passengers. When a severe storm happened and threatened the vessel commanded by Captain Bennett, he ordered the death of a woman named Catherine Grady, all because she was a "witch at sea."

Ten years later, a letter in the *English State* papers mentioned, "the anticipated loss of a British ship with all on board, because two witches sat in the maintop and could not be dislodged."

A minister, David Lindsay, accused William Harding of practicing the black arts. This happened in Northumberland County in 1656. William received ten lashes from a whip upon his bare back and was banished forever from the county within two months.

A record filed in Westmoreland County in 1694 reported that Phyllis Money was accused of casting a spell over Henry Dunkin's horse, plus teaching witchcraft to her daughter, who also happened to be Dunkin's wife. She was also accused of teaching Dunkin himself to be a wizard. The accused countersued, but it appears neither side won. A year later, Henry Dunkin accused John Dunkin and his wife, Elizabeth, of practicing the dark arts. Henry made claims that Elizabeth was regularly sucked by the Devil. If this charge had been proven, most times in the Colonies, the accused witch would be hung by the neck until dead. Instead, Elizabeth sued Henry and was awarded forty pounds.

In 1695, in King and Queen County, William Morris sued a woman for accusing his wife of witchcraft. The jury found the woman guilty of defamation and Morris and his wife were awarded five hundred pounds of tobacco.

In 1838, a man named March lived on a hill not far from Abingdon. He was considered to be honest and industrious. When he became afflicted with scrofula in the most severe way, the belief was that it was the effects of a spell or pow-wow conducted by Yates, who lived in the neighborhood and was believed to be a conjurer or wizard.

March called for an Indian doctor and instead if being cured grew worse, so he took matters into his own hands. He would kill the wizard by sketching a rude likeness of Yates upon a tree, then fired at it repeatedly with bullets containing silver.

It didn't work, for Yates appeared unaffected. Marsh decided to shoot the original with a musket, using two silver-laced balls. He waited for his opportunity and took it when Yates walked down the road and passed him by. Both balls entered the back of Yates's neck.

Yates survived the ambush, and Marsh was sent to the penitentiary.

The most famous witch of Virginia is Grace Sherwood of Pungo in Virginia Beach. Though many legends surround her, she was a real person who wasn't really a witch.

I arrived on the morning of Grace Sherwood Day, July 12, 2008, for the reenactment of her ducking. There were to be two that day, one at 9 am and the second one at 10 am. After that, there would be events at Ferry Plantation for the day. Danielle Sheets, the daughter of Belinda Nash who was the Director of Ferry Plantation, played Grace. A boat was rowed to the dock where Danielle along with others playing the magistrate, jurors, and spectators from the trial climbed down into it. I watched as they rowed away to Witchduck Point, taking photos of it all with my camera.

Later, I had an interview with Belinda Nash about Grace. Grace was born in 1660, and was an only child. With no sons to help him, her father taught her how to work the land and how to irrigate it well. She knew how to make things grow, and from her mother, before she died when Grace was young, she learned how to be a midwife. She couldn't read or write, but she could memorize well. Grace could swim well, too, and in those days, the only people who could swim were sailors' sons. A woman wasn't supposed to be able to swim.

She married James Sherwood and they had three sons, James, John, and Richard. She grew cotton (for cottonseed oil, nothing more), rice, and tobacco. Unlike the other women of the day, who stayed indoors and did womanly things, she would go outside to work the land and even visited the Indians, learning about herbs from them, which she also grew on the plantation. This brought suspicion upon her. It didn't help that she was very attractive in a physical way, either. Joseph F. Filipowski, who built the boat used for the reenactment on Grace Sherwood Day, told me that the local magistrate had tried to seduce her and she had refused his attentions.

It also didn't help that the neighbors accused her of blighting gardens, causing livestock to die, and influencing the weather. When a neighbor had blighted cotton and the Sherwoods did not, that was because of Grace's knowledge of irrigation, but not witchcraft. It didn't matter. Suddenly, people began to whisper things about her—that if someone saw a firefly at night, it was actually Grace dancing in the moonlight. After Grace was accused of bewitching a neighbor's crop in 1698, allegations kept growing over time until the Princess Anne County government and her accusers decided she would be tested by ducking. When the sheriff searched Grace's house (which no longer stands today), there was no evidence of a witch ball, which made her a possible witch all the more in her accusers' eyes.

The reason witches were ducked was because water was considered pure and would not permit a witch to sink into its depths. Based on this theory, the accused was tied up and thrown into the water. If the person drowned, he was declared innocent of witchcraft; if he could stay afloat until he could free himself, he was declared a witch. In this case, innocent, damned, guilty, damned—you might die either way.

Grace was tried in the second Princess Anne County Courthouse, found guilty, and consented to the traditional trial by water. One of the many tall tales that have been handed down from generation to generation has to do with the day of her ducking. On July 10, 1706, at 10 am, her accusers tied her thumbs to her big toes cross-bound and dropped her into the western branch of the Lynnhaven River near what is now known as Witchduck Point. When they led Grace Sherwood through the crowd that had turned out to see her put into the water, she told them, "All right, all of you po' white trash, you've worn out your shoes traipsin' here to see me ducked, but before you'll get back home again you are goin' to get the duckin' of your life." When they put Grace into the water the sky was as bright blue as a bird's wing, but immediately afterward, it grew pitch black, thunder rolled and the lightning flashed across the heavens. The terrified people bolted for home, only to be washed off the roads and into the ditches by a regular cloudburst. In reality, Grace couldn't have walked, being tied as she was, and when placed in the water, Grace

Reenactment of Grace Sherwood's trial and ducking.

did not drown but floated, which was considered a sign of guilt. Most likely the ties came undone so she could swim, which she could do well. She was imprisoned for seven years and ten months. Released in 1714, Grace paid the back taxes on her property and returned to her farm, where she worked the land until her death at eighty years of age in September, 1740.

Her story doesn't end there, for on July 10, 2006, after Belinda Nash worked hard for seven years to get Grace pardoned, Governor Timothy M. Kaine fully exonerated Grace. She is the only deceased person known to be cleared in Virginia. A statute was unveiled on Saturday, April 21, 2007, on the lawn of Bayside Hospital in Virginia Beach. It was placed near the corner of Independence Boulevard and North Witchduck Road, within two tenths of a mile of the old second Princess Anne Courthouse of 1706.

I got to see the statue that afternoon when I left Ferry Plantation after the interview with Belinda. Three other people stopped by to look at it and were reading the inscriptions on each side of the pedestal where the statue stood when I drove up. The sunlight sparkled from behind it as I tried to take photographs of the statue and the words on the pedestal. The bright light from behind the statue might have come from Grace herself, the glow of her goodness showing. Whatever the case, it was a fitting end to Grace Sherwood's Day.

The statue of Grace Sherwood in Virginian Beach.

Witches in Western and Southwestern Virginia

In the *History of the Valley,* written by Samuel Kercheval in the 1830s, he stated: "The belief in Witchcraft was prevalent among the early settlers of the western portion of Virginia. Not only women as witches, but men considered as wizards (also know as witch doctors)."

Wizards were men possessed of the same malevolent powers as the witches, except they seldom exercised them for bad purposes. Their power was used most times for the purpose of counteracting the influence of the witches of the opposite sex.

One way people in western part of Virginia broke a witch's spell was by drawing a picture of the witch on a stump or piece of bread and shooting at it with a silver bullet. Another method was to take the urine of a person who'd been cursed, corked it up in a vial, then hang it up in a chimney. This complicated the witch with a strangury, which lasted as long as the vial remained in the chimney. The only way a witch could relieve herself, would be to borrow something from the family she had placed the spell on.

To get rid of a spell placed on cattle or dogs, the animals were branded on the forehead with a branding iron, or if dead, burned until nothing but ashes remained. This inflicted a spell upon the witch, and the only way she could remove it was, again, by borrowing something belonging to the accursed.

To milk cows, witches would place a new pin in a new towel and affix the towel over the doorway. Using incantations, the witch could extract the milk from the towel in the same manner of milking a cow, without actually doing it. This was the reason used when cows were too poor to give milk.

Beliefs like this went on into the 1930-40s when interviewers combed the hills of western Virginia to talk to the people and collect the folklore. There are still some who live in the southwest portion of the state who believe in the lore of witches.

One such place is Witch Mountain. It is a few miles northeast of Hillsville, the county seat of Carroll County, off Route 221 near Galax. It is said that a sect that believes in witches and maybe even practices witchcraft themselves inhabits it. There are those who fear it and always take a path leading along the base by the safe light of the sun. Some that travel at night go out miles out of their way to avoid it.

One tale of witchcraft happened near Bristol, involving a settler that owned a flock of sheep. The animals began to die and no reason could be found. Worried that they had been bewitched, he contacted a local witch doctor for help. The witch doctor told him to go home, skin out a shoulder of one of the lambs, and bake it in an oven. While doing this, he was not to allow anyone into the house, or let anyone borrow or steal anything from the house.

The man did everything the witch doctor told him to do. Two hours later, a neighbor woman dropped by, wanting to borrow some meal. When refused, she asked for some water, but she was told they hadn't brought any water up to the house that day. She went away.

The woman returned, walking toward the house faster than before. She seemed agitated and couldn't keep still. After asking what the man was baking in the oven, she even tried to overturn it.

Then she took off, but came back minutes later to point at the oven and scream, "For God's sake, take that out of there! You're killing me! Just look!" She ripped the sleeve of her blouse off and the man saw her own shoulder as crispy brown as the mutton shoulder.

Another tale concerned a lamb. A woman and her husband had a ewe that died after giving birth to two lambs. The husband got another ewe to take one lamb, but couldn't get it to take the other one. He gave that lamb to his wife to take care of. One morning it was off its food and she put it outside thinking that maybe it would graze. Instead, it stumbled, butting into things as if it were blind.

A witch doctor came by to borrow an axe and when he saw the lamb, told her it was bewitched. He told her to put a plow share in the fire and before it got red-hot to take it out. Then she must pour cold spring water over it to cool it in a hurry or the witch might die.

Soon after she did all as the witch doctor told her to, there a rapping sounded at her front door. It was Kate Upp, who lived halfway up the side of Witch Mountain. Kate wanted to borrow her wool cards, but the woman lied and said another neighbor had borrowed them.

Kate sat down and complained of feeling faint and needing water. She even asked for the door to be opened a crack. Just then the lamb scrambled to its feet and came over to nuzzle her owner. Knowing this meant it was all right, she dragged the plow share out of the coals and poured cold water over it. Kate left afterwards. Later, Kate was found dead, just off the path leading up the mountain. The woman wondered if she had left the plow share in the fire too long.

There is another story set in Springfield, about a woman, Mrs. Trennis, accused of being a witch and connected to a treasure. Mrs. Trennis kept to herself and sold ginger cakes and cider to both local residents and to those passing through on stagecoaches.

She hoarded gold, silver, and copper coins, squirreling it all away in an old kettle that she hid under a loose board in her kitchen-bedroom. When she grew too old to care for herself, her ten-year-old nephew did so. One winter night, she arose from bed, pried up the loose board, and took out the kettle. She carried it outside, returning without it to collapse on her bed. The next morning the nephew found her dead.

Over time, people would move into the house, then move out not long after. They spoke of being frightened by an apparition of the old woman. The house was torn down and still the old woman would be seen, dissipating right where the house had been. As for the hidden money, no one has ever found it.

Oak Hill Road in Danville is considered a gravity road. This means that it's suppose to draw you up it. There's a story that a church and many religious people lived alongside of it. A witch moved there to torment them. In righteous anger, the people had her hung and left her body there for all to see. They put up crosses all around the land so it would be blessed again, then went about their business.

The legend goes on to say that the witch haunts the road and that she will try to yank you toward where her house had stood. The reason that is given is so she can kill you for what the religious people had done to her. There are those who claim this weird phenomenon really does happen and that it scared them so badly, they won't ever drive on the road again. Is there a witch's ghost behind this or just some strange funhouse effect? I couldn't find anything to substantiate the story.

The next time you go for a drive into the lonely Virginian country late at night, stare through your front windshield and you just might see something fly pass the moon above. It may not be a bat or owl. It may be a witch. Just make sure you keep a witch ball or witch bottle handy in the glove compartment.

Chapter Thirty-Two
Yo Ho Ho!
Pirates Tales of Virginia

"Now and then we had a hope that if we lived and were good, God would permit us to be pirates."

~Mark Twain

No matter what the movie *Pirates of the Caribbean* says, pirates have also been seen along the Eastern seaboard from Florida to New England. There have been myths and legends told about them in the Old Dominion.

Because valuable cargoes traveled through the Chesapeake Bay, trade in Virginia often came to a standstill when pirates patrolled sea lanes and threatened vessels could not leave the safety of ports. During one six-week period, not a single ship dared to leave the safety of Virginia shores. Edward Teach, Blackbeard, as he was more known as, was the main cause of this maritime panic. Using a summit, now referred to as Blackbeard's Hill, the pirate and his watchmen had an open view of the Chesapeake Bay, which the British navy ineffectively protected.

Blackbeard has inspired a Pirate Festival here in Hampton that usually happens the first weekend in June. You can find out more about this festival at http://www.blackbeardpiratefestival.com/.

Blackbeard's Skull

Author Deborah Painter told me a legend about Blackbeard, the pirate. He was killed off the shores of North Carolina and his head was brought back to Hampton to be suspended from a pole on a pier at Sunset Creek, just a mile from where Ms. Painter works. The story goes on to say that, to this day, the decapitated pirate searches for his head in the Chesapeake Bay.

One evening Blackbeard moored his ship at the mouth of the Potomac River and went ashore. There were two parties. One was to procure provisions, the other to assist in secreting their treasures. An English sloop-of-war followed him and dropped anchor in just the right spot to prevent him from escaping. A manned barge was sent to capture his ship.

Blackbeard and his men went back to their ship. The commander of the men who boarded the ship was a Scotsman who desired the honor of subduing Teach himself. The men battled by sword. The Scot felled a strong blow upon the pirate's shoulders, causing blood to flow.

"Ha!" said Blackbeard, "well struck, brother seaman."

The Scot gave a reply, then with his next stroke, separated Teach's head from his shoulders.

The Scot ordered that the head be boiled in boiling water and thoroughly cleansed. As a sign to other pirates, Blackbeard's head was hung from the bow of a ship. Meanwhile, his corpse was simply thrown overboard. Then, the head was hung on a pole and placed at a point on the James River, also known as Blackbeard's Point. When the Scot went ashore, he made a present of Blackbeard's skull to the governor of the Virginia colony. Then the legend says that the skull was tipped with silver to become a drinking vessel.

Today, Ocracoke, with its history of piracy and maritime warfare is now a quiet island famous for vacationing tourists. The citizens of Ocracoke still continue to speak in the old English dialect, known as brogue. According to legend, Blackbeard's skull cup still exists around the island, even spurring accounts of locals and visitors sipping from the skull of the South's deadliest pirate.

Buccaneers at Carter's Grove

There is a myth that three pirates were buried in the cellar at Carter's Grove. It is also said that their ghosts still hold a card game there, every now and then.

Old House Woods in Mathews County

There is a story about Blackbeard involved with the hauntings of Old House Woods. It is said that he killed other pirates burying a treasure there in the seventeenth century. You can read more about this in the Freaky Legends of Old House Woods chapter.

Buried Treasure of Blackbeard and Other Pirates on Assateague

Blackbeard and other pirates reportedly sailed the waters around Assateague Island and used the island as a hideout and as a place to bury their treasure. Whether it is true or not, standing on the island and looking out to sea makes the tales almost believable. One can breathe in the salt from the sea and hear the seagulls as they scream while soaring overhead. As I swept my gaze to the sea and watched a couple of ponies standing in the beach, I almost swore I could see a ghostly pirate ship forging through the white-capped waves. Then the vision vanished as I snapped some photos with my camera.

If Blackbeard or any of his cohorts had buried their ill-gotten gains somewhere on the island, then only they, the ponies, and the seagulls know where for sure. For none has ever been found.

Chapter Thirty-Three
Native American Myths
and Legends

It wouldn't be a Virginian legends, myths, and true tales book without the Native Americans. They, even now, still live here, and there are also those tribes that have lived here in the past, but have now moved on.

When the white man arrived in Virginia, there were three big groups of Woodland Indians living here. These were the Siouan, Algonquian, and the Iroquois.

Today there are eight tribes and two small reservations in Virginia. The register shows 2,500 people. Census figures show another 15,000 people of Indian ancestry living across Virginia. Two tribes, the Pamunkey and the Mattaponi, have small reservations in King William County. Six other incorporated groups are officially recognized as Indian tribes by the Commonwealth of Virginia, though not by the federal government. These are the Chickahominy Indian Tribe in Charles City County; Chickahominy Indian Tribe, Eastern Division, in New Kent County; Monacan Indian Tribe in Amherst County; Nansemond Indian Tribal Association in the City of Chesapeake; Rappahannock Indian Tribe in Essex, Caroline, and King and Queen Counties; and the Upper Mattaponi Indian Tribe in King William County. If you wish to learn more about the various tribes, go to this Web site at http://indians.vipnet.org/tribes.cfm.

The Monacan

The Siouan lived in different parts of Virginia. The term Siouan is the adjective denoting the "Sioux" Indians and cognate tribes. The word "Sioux" has been variously and vaguely used. Originally, it was a corruption of a term expressing enmity or contempt, applied to a part of the plains tribes by the forest-dwelling Algonquian Indians. One of these tribes was the Monacan.

Their culture was very similar to that of the Powathan. They combined farming, hunting, fishing, and gathering for their food and materials. The women made household items out of wood, bone, animal skins, and other locally available resources.

Monacans mined copper which they wore in necklaces. Copper beads were a sign of wealth and high status.

They traded with other Indian tribes. They traded copper, which was highly valued, furs, and dyes for items such as shell beads. Monacans made baskets with animal and flower designs. They used the thread they made from milkweed to make a strong cord to make the baskets. In addition, they made pottery using the coil method to create beautiful and durable pottery.

There are few written records about the Monacans. They were not interested in dealing with the English, unlike the Powhatans. A number of English explorers visited Monacan towns and described them, but none remained to learn the Monacan languages, and thus the historical record of these people is poor in contrast to Powhatan history.

The Monacan tribe used steam to help cure some kinds of sickness. They built special huts covered with clay to hold in the steam. They would heat coals and then pour water on the coals to make the steam. We call this a "sauna." They greased their bodies with bear oil. Early visitors thought they were a healthy and handsome people.

The Monacan tribe, like many Siouan-speaking tribes, buried the bones of people who died in earth-covered mounds. The bones of many people were buried together. The Cherokees and the Powhatans did not do this.

Next is a legend about the Natural Bridge in Natural Bridge, Virginia, in Rockbridge County, and the Monacan Indians. The legend came from the Natural Bridge Web site at http://www.naturalbridgeva.com/bridge.html.

The Legend of the Monacan Indians and Natural Bridge

According to legend, the Monacan Indians discovered the Natural Bridge while under attack by Algonquin tribes. When they reached the chasm of Cedar Creek and discovered no visible way to cross over, they prayed for the Great Spirit to protect them. Just as they arose from praying, a 215-foot-tall bridge appeared. Women and children crossed to safety. The men followed but not until after they met and defeated the Algonquins.

Higher than Niagara Falls, Natural Bridge is one of the oldest tourist destinations in the United States. It has been included in several "Seven Natural Wonders of the New World" lists, mainly in the nineteenth and early twentieth centuries. It is a National Historic Landmark, a Virginia Historic Landmark, and is listed in the National Register of Historic Places. Two hundred and fifteen feet high, it is forty feet thick, with the arch having a span of ninety feet. U.S. Route 11 still passes over it.

One of the seven natural wonders of the New World—Natural Bridge.

I visited the reproduction of the Monacan village from centuries ago when we went to Natural Bridge August 28, 2008. Two Monacan women were there, one of them weaving a basket just like her ancestors did. It was interesting. My husband and I walked into the various buildings. I snapped pictures, both in black and white and color. Interestingly enough, I caught a couple of orbs in the one with the fire going. There were the only orbs I got when we went to the Natural Bridge. What does this mean? Are Native Americans still hanging around, maybe even giving approval to their descendents for doing this?

As for the bridge itself, it was awe-inspiring, and an incredible feeling overcame me as I stared at it. Touching the rock, I imagined George Washington when he surveyed it in 1750, and dared to scale up its side to carve his initials in it. As I read the signs along the way to the end where a waterfall waited, I learned of the legend of the Lost River. There had been several unsuccessful attempts to locate the underground channels of the river. Colored dyes and floatation devices had been used. All failed to determine the source of the final destination of this underground river. Though there is no doubt it goes from Natural Bridge Caverns to under the bridge itself.

The history tells us that it was discovered about 1812, when men from Saltpetre Cave heard its rushing waters and blasted the opening, attached a water main in there to transport water to hoppers and kettles used to extract nitrate from the cave.

The Algonquian

One of the Algonquian tribes is the Powhatan, which everyone would know for the Pocahontas and John Smith story, since she came from this tribe. They were the most powerful Algonquians at the time the white man came. Chief Powhatan, Pocahontas's father, offered a hand of friendship to the first settlers. There were thirty different tribes of Indians in the Powhatan Confederacy, 10,000 when the colonists arrived in Virginia. The Algonquian lived mainly around the Chesapeake Bay and its surrounding rivers. The Powhatan built their homes out of saplings, with a hole at the top of the frame to allow smoke from their fires to escape. They kept a fire going all of the time. Most people would imagine that this was for cooking or warmth, but they did this due to a superstition. They believed that evil spirits would come into their homes if they let their fires die.

Powhatan

There is a story connected to Chief Powhatan himself. It concerns the "Powhatan Stone." It is said that the Powhatan Seat is supposed to be where Tree Hill Farm is now, a mile or so outside of Richmond city limits on Route 5. But others dispute this, claiming that Powathan ruled from what is now known as Fulton Hill. The Stone itself can be seen today, just outside the Chimborazo Medical Museum in Church Hill, in the area that overlooks Bloody Run.

The Powhatan Stone.

Curse of the Three Sisters—Northern Virginia

Another tale of the Algonquian tribes is about a curse by three Algonquin women that apparently seems to still work today. This curse concerns three large granite rocks that rise out of the water between Virginia's shoreline and Washington, D.C. The story takes place a hundred years before Jamestown was settled by the white man.

Though the land was rich with farmland and game and everyone did well, peace did not reign here. To the north were the Iroquois and Susquehannocks and they would raid the Algonquin tribes of the Powhatan Confederacy in the Virginia area, the battles fierce and bloody.

After a long siege, one Powhatan chief felt it was safe enough for his warriors and him to hunt for food. He'd forbidden, though, three of his young sons to go with them, feeling they were not old enough to defend themselves if trouble came.

The young men decided to show their father how well they could go out and bring enough fresh fish to feed the women, children, and old men in the village. They did this after the hunting party left.

Now the greatest abundance of fish lived in the waters near the northern shore where the Susquehannocks warriors might still be. Using a canoe, they pushed it into the river and struck out. Not long after, a Susquehannock scouting party captured them and they were brought before the village, tortured, and killed. Of the villagers, three young daughters of the village shaman who were in love with the young men watched with horror and growing anger.

They devised among themselves that they would cross the river to the village of the Susquehannocks to demand the warriors who'd killed the men they loved. They would take them back to their village to beguile them with their beauty and their fathers' medicine. But afterwards, they would kill them by a long, agonizing death.

The sisters lashed several logs into a raft and pushed it from shore. But the current from the river proved too strong and fast, and soon, they found themselves racing downstream. Still angry over the senseless deaths of the men they loved, the sisters cursed the river and said if they couldn't cross it, no one would ever be able to do so.

The raft broke up and they sank to their deaths. The curse became true as one flash from a lightening struck the spot where they went down. That night the storm continued and the river's waters went crazy. The following morning all grew calm as the sun rose into the sky. But three boulders had risen out of the spot where the sisters drowned, boulders that hadn't been there before.

From that time on, the rocks take their toll on those who dare to try to cross the river there. A growing list of those victims who died is added to by local law enforcement—many fishermen, swimmers and boaters. Old-timers claim that you can hear moaning over the Potomac during a storm, warning of another impending drowning.

In 1972, when they tried to construct a bridge to span the river, it became interrupted by one of the worse storms ever. Whitecaps surged on the water and lightening struck the spot where the bridge supports were beginning to be built. The water surged and swept away the construction framework. Funny thing, the bridge was to be called "Three Sisters Bridge."

Next time you feel you want to test an Indian curse, try swimming in the Potomac where three sisters once died.

The Iroquois—Cherokee, Meherrin, and Nottaway Tribes

The Iroquois had three tribes in Virginia, with 2,500 members. These were the Cherokee, the Meherrin, and the Nottoway tribes. They all lived in the southern area of the state. Enjoy this Cherokee tale of how the Earth came to be.

Earth Making—Cherokee Indians

In the beginning, water covered everything. Living creatures existed, but their homes were up there, above the rainbow, and it was crowded.

The animals complained, "We are jammed together and we need more room."

To find out what existed under the water, Water Beetle was sent to scout it out.

Water Beetle skimmed over the surface, but not finding any solid foothold, he dove to the bottom. Scooping up a dab of soft mud, he brought it back up. Like magic, the mud spread out in the four directions. It became the earth. Then Someone Powerful connected it to the sky with cords.

In the beginning the earth was flat, soft, and moist. Eager to see if it had dried enough to live on, the animals sent out the birds to find out. The birds would come back and say there was no spot they could perch on.

The animals sent Grandfather Buzzard then. He flew close, saw that the earth was still soft, but noticed the mud hardening in the Cherokee land. But Grandfather Buzzard had grown tired and lagging, and when he flapped his wings downward, they made a valley where they touched the earth. And when he swept his wings upward, they made a mountain. The animals peeped down from above the rainbow and exclaimed, "If he keeps going, we will have nothing but mountains!" That is why the Cherokee land has so many mountains.

Finally the earth grew dry and hard enough. The animals descended upon it. They could not see well since there was no sun or moon. So one of them said, "Grab the Sun from up there behind the rainbow and pull him down too."

As they yanked the Sun down, they said to it, "This is the road you follow."

The road stretched from east to west, and that gave sunrise and sunset.

They had light, but it was too hot, as the Sun hovered close to the earth. The crawfish had his back sticking out of a stream and the Sun burned it red. This spoiled his meat forever and the people still won't eat crawfish.

Everyone begged sorcerers and shamans to raise the Sun higher. They pushed him up as high as a man, but it was still too hot. So they pushed him higher, but still, not far enough. They did this four times, making him finally the height of four men and since this was just hot enough, satisfied, they left him alone.

Before making humans, Someone Powerful created plants and animals and told them to stay awake. They had to watch for seven days and seven nights. But many of the animals and plants couldn't do it. Some fell asleep after one day. Others, after three. Only the owl and the mountain lion remained awake after seven days and nights. That is why, to this day, they have the gift of being able to see in the dark so they can hunt at night.

As for the plants, only the cedar, pine, holly, and laurel stayed awake to the eighth day. Someone Powerful said, "Because you watched and kept awake as you have been told, you will not lose your hair in the winter." That is why these plants and trees remain green all year long.

After the animals and plants had been created, Someone Powerful made a man and his sister. The man poked her with a fish and told her to give birth. Seven days later, she gave birth to a baby, and another seven days later, another child was born. Every seven days she gave birth. Humans began to increase rapidly. Someone Powerful thought there would be no more room on the earth, and arranged that a woman could only have a child every year. And that's how it is.

Legend of the White Deer—Great Dismal Swamp, Chesapeake

There is another local Indian tale told that is set in the Great Dismal Swamp of the Tidewater region. It is one of tragic love. There had been an Indian maiden, Wa-Cheagles, who happened to be daughter of the chief of one of two warring tribes in the area. For years she had an interesting relationship with a doe that she called Cin-Co, which meant guiding friend. It was believed that Cin-Co brought deer into the swamp each autumn. The doe would always lead her current fawn up to Wa-Cheagles to show her, at the edge of the forest near a pool of dark brown water. This was the only way for the squaw to meet with the doe as squaws were not allowed into the forest because the tribes believed this to be an evil omen.

One year, Cin-Co appeared alone, limping. She walked back into the forest, doing it two to three times, until Wa-Cheagles overcame her fear and followed her. The doe lead her to her fawn that had a hoof firmly on a barely living rattlesnake. No doubt this reptile had bitten Cin-Co and was the reason for her limp. The doe was telling the Indian maiden she wanted her to care for her fawn, since the doe was dying from the rattlesnake poison. While there, Wa-Cheagles heard a moan and discovered an Indian brave from an enemy tribe with a swollen leg from a rattlesnake bite. If she attended to him, she must pledge herself to him. Both then would be hunted down, to be killed by arrows with tips laced with water moccasin venom.

But she went ahead and helped him, removing her beret and tying it around his leg. Using some snakeroot she found, she applied a poultice over the wound. Ready to leave, she saw that Cin-Co had died and the fawn had vanished. Upset, she went back to her tribe.

For three days, she would sneak away to tend to the brave. On the third day, her father appeared in the clearing, finding not only her, but the brave, too. He carried away Cin-Co's carcass, giving them enough time to get away.

Wa-Cheagles and her lover stopped at Lake Drummond to rest. Just then, three warriors from her tribe confronted them, determined to erase the curse from their tribe.

As the warriors drew back their bows to send their arrows flying, a dark cloud blotted out the sun and a loud rustling noise filled the air. A flock of wild geese flew around Wa-Cheagles and her lover. The geese settled en masse on the lake until not one inch of the water could be seen. Terrified, the braves dropped their bows and arrows and bolted.

Just then, the "swamp spirit" rose out of the lake and strolled over the backs of the geese, approaching the two lovers. It told them that Cin-Co's spirit had saved them; that Wa-Cheagles must continue the doe's good work. The spirit magicked the maiden into a white deer, a small crimson spot on her forehead. Her lover became a charmed hunter. The spirit told them they would roam the swamp's forest forever, side by side, protected from both animals and hunters by rattlesnakes.

To this day there are hunters and others who say they have seen the white deer and the Indian brave by her side. Whenever a hunter pursues them, a rattlesnake appears on the spot they had been sighted, hissing and rattling its rattle.

Legend of Bloody Run—Richmond

In 1656, the bloodiest Native American battle had been fought near the falls of the James River in what is now Richmond. Six to seven hundred members of the Shackoconian tribe of the Manahoac Confederacy had decided to move there in their search for a new dwelling place. The English Colonists did not want this and, joined by the Pamunkey tribe under Totopotomoi, they met them in battle. Colonel Edward Hill led the Colonial Rangers and Totopotomoi led a hundred warriors in what we now call the Battle of Bloody Run.

There's a legend behind this that so many had been slain (Totopotomoi included), that their blood flooded the spring. In the end, Hill became disgusted with it and had to pay for the cost of the battle and was stripped of his rank. Years later, the bloodiest Civil War battle happened at this very creek, again running blood into it.

Bloody Run.

Chapter Thirty-Four
Virginian African-American Stories

Most African Americans are the descendants of captive Africans held in the United States from 1619 to 1865. The first African slaves were brought to Jamestown, Virginia in 1619. The English settlers treated these captives as indentured servants and released them after a number of years. This practice was gradually replaced by a form of race-based slavery used in the Caribbean. Freed, theses former slaves became competition for property and income. Even more so, released servants had to be replaced. But making others into forced servants led to bringing back Africans as slaves. Massachusetts became the first colony to legalize slavery in 1641. Other colonies followed not long after, passing laws that made the children of slaves and non-Christian imported servants slaves for life.

African American folktales have origins rooted in West African literary and cultural forms of expression. When Africans were taken from their homeland and brought to America as slaves, they also brought with them their individual cultures, languages, and customs. However, their white slaveholders tried to suppress this part of their heritage. Thus, they had to find other ways of expression, mainly storytelling and songs. Folktales and spirituals arose from the life on the plantations, mingled with the memories and customs the slaves brought with them from Africa. These stories used acting, gesturing, and singing—elevating storytelling into an art.

Most slave owners forbade their slaves from speaking their own language, and forced them to speak English. They also forbid the slaves to learn to read and write. It was believed that by keeping their slaves ignorant, there would be no rebellions or uprisings.

But the slave spirituals were means of communicating discontent, homelessness, and exile.

Not all songs were of disparity and loss; some expressed love, joy, and hope. Some even taught lessons or gave explanations for why certain things were the way they were. Many showed how to outsmart those who kept them down or tried to own their souls as much as their bodies. And some were stories for no other reason than for enjoyment.

Why Dogs Chase Cats

Once upon a time, Dog married Cat and both were happy together. When Dog got home from work each night, Cat would say she was too sick to make him dinner. Dog didn't mind at first, but eventually, he got tired of fixing dinner after a hard day of work. In his opinion, she stayed home all day.

One day, he told her he was off to work. Instead, he hid in a cupboard to see if she was really ill. As soon as Cat knew he was gone, she started to play some games with Kitten. They laughed and ran about and Cat didn't act sick at all.

Dog burst of the cupboard. When Cat saw him, she stuck a marble in her cheek and claimed to have a toothache. Angry with her, Dog chased her all around the house.

Since then, Dogs chase Cats.

Malindy and the Little Devil

There once was a child named Malindy, who loved to sing and dance. Wherever she went, she would sing, "I'm going to get me some milk from the moo-moo-cow." While she sang, she danced this way and that.

One time, as she walked along the fence line carrying her pail full of warm milk, she tripped on a rough spot on the path. Because of this, her pail spilled milk over the ground and over herself, too.

Crying, she sang, "Oh boo-hoo, poor me. Now Papa will punish me and I'll get no supper, too. Boo-hoo-hoo!"

Something furry all over and with a long tail skipped along the top rail of the fence up to her. Malindy thought it was a baboon and asked what it was doing there. It didn't answer and then she saw it holding a pitchfork.

"I know you," she cried harder. "You're a devil."

The devil replied, "Now, now. I won't hurt you."

She stopped crying. "You're a tiny fellow."

"They call me Little Devil, but I know how to change. And he grew to giant size, blotting out the trees.

"You're something awful!"

The Devil agreed. "That I am. But listen. I'm just starting out with devilment. This will be my first time with a child and I want to help you."

When she told him she was listening, he said, "I'll restore your milk to its pail for a price."

"Will you dry off my dress too? 'Cause my mama will spank me for getting it dirty."

"I can do that," Little Devil agreed. "First, though, you must promise to give me your soul when you pass beyond this earth."

"I want to stay here a long time."

"How long?"

Since she wanted to be as old as her mother someday, she answered, "Twenty-nine years!"

Little Devil said, "I can do that for you, Malindy. I'll restore your milk, fix your dress, and give you twenty-nine years, too. But at the end of that time, you will give me your soul."

"Deal."

"Well, let's dance then," said Little Devil.

Both danced and pranced all along the path. As they did, the pail up-righted with milk inside it. Malindy's dress dried and looked good as new.

Malindy twirled around as Little Devil spun her.

They parted and time flew by until, one day, Malindy was twenty-nine years old. Grown up now, with children of her own, she had forgotten about Little Devil and her promise to it. A commotion erupted in the air and everything turned red and black and all bright. A voice hollered, "I'm going to come after you. I'm coming after you. Right now!" And Little Devil appeared out of nowhere, right before her.

Suddenly, Malindy remembered. "I remember you, no bigger than a minute. How are you doing?"

"Doing just fine. I came for your soul like you promised me."

She nodded. "Yes. Let me get it for you."

She turned her back to him and tore the sole of her shoe off.

Then she turned around and handed it over to Little Devil.

"This is it?" Little Devil asked.

"Sure is."

He frowned. "I thought it would be bigger."

"That's it," she said.

Not knowing any better, the ugly little devil took her sole to his master.

As for Malindy, she went dancing through life after that. So did her many children. They all lived happily ever after. Because the devil can only get your *sole* but one time. After that, he has to quit.

That's all.

The Old Plantation Master's Ghost

After Robert Edward's death, there were parties after parties held on his plantation. Loads of riotous living and money squandered like water through fingers. One night, the wine gave out so a slave was sent to the cellar to get some more. The slave saw a man pacing back and forth in the road. Frightened, the slave bolted to the wine cellar. When he ran back to the house, the man followed him. And when the slave reached the steps of the Big House, the man caught up with him and grabbed him by the arm. The slave looked up into the face of the man and saw his old master. For years after that, it was said that anyone could see the marks left on the slave's arm as proof that he saw his old master.

Chapter Thirty-Five
Civil War Myths and Legends

"War is sorrowful, but there is one thing infinitely more horrible than the worst horrors of war, and that is the feeling that nothing is worth fighting for..."

~Harper's Weekly, December 31, 1864

The Civil War, also known as the War Between the States, occurred 1861-1865. More Americans died during this conflict than in the Revolutionary War, Spanish-American War, the War of 1812, the Mexican War, the Indian Wars, World War I and World War II, and the Korean conflict. Brothers from the same family would go off to war, one fighting for the North, the other for the South. Three million fought—600,000 paid the ultimate price for freedom.

With all the horror of brutal death and brother against brother, a war like this can cause hauntings, many of them real. But along with the true stories are the myths and folklore that gets thrown in. And there are even true stories so bizarre that you'd think they weren't real, but they actually are.

Ominous Signs of the Impending Civil War

Psychic in nature, there were portents or signs, warning of the approaching War Between the States. As mentioned by L. B. Taylor Jr. in his book, *Civil War Ghosts of Virginia,* there may have even been a precognitive vision by George Washington himself. This vision took place when he was camped with his men at Valley Forge in 1777. Washington told Anthony Sherman that he saw a "singularly beautiful being" in his tent one night.

Washington could feel the atmosphere in his tent grow luminous and full of sensations. He felt like he was dying, able to experience what he imagined accompanies death. He saw manifestations of black clouds, lightning bolts, lights of a thousand suns, thunder of cannons, along with cries of many in mortal combat. At that moment the figure vanished.

Some have interpreted this as a premonition of the Civil War. But no one can be ever sure.

The next omen happened in April 1861. A comet soared in the skies over Washington and Northern Virginia at the time. A family in the area had an old African slave named Oola. The other slaves were afraid of her "evil eye" and claimed that her piercing eyes sent shivers to whoever looked into them. They said she could conjure spells also.

When the comet flashed across the skies, she gave a dire prediction. Calling it a "great fire sword," she went on to say a great war approached. The handle pointed to the North while the point of it pinpointed the South. She went on to say that the North would take this sword and cut out the heart of the South. If Lincoln took the sword, though, he would expire due to it.

The last omen occurred on June 29, 1861. A new Union flag was raised at a ceremony at the White House. Federal generals and their aides attended, along with members of the cabinet and other guests.

As the Marine band began to play the National Anthem and the guests rose from their seats, and while the officers saluted, Abraham Lincoln took the cord to raise the flag. Nothing happened. Lincoln tried again, but this time he pulled harder. The Union flag's upper corner tore and hung down. Gasps of horror filled the room and one general became very disturbed by the incident.

The Carbine—Abingdon

There's a story about a man named John Dick Adams. He became captain of a company of some sort of home guards. One day, both his company and a company of Yankee home guards got into a skirmish. John was shot through one arm, then one of his legs.

As mentioned in the Blood Stain chapter, there was a young Confederate soldier—John Dick Adams—in Abingdon who had to carry some important papers about the location of the Union army to Robert E. Lee. At the time, he was in love with a young woman who went to Martha Washington College, which is now Martha Washington Inn.

He had to say farewell to his lady love and traveled through the cave system underlying Abington. He snuck up a secret stairway and entered the college. But just as he was with the woman, two Union soldiers came up the stairs and discovered them. They fired at him and the soldier fell, his blood staining the floor. (It can still be seen today. Even when carpets are put over it, holes would mysteriously appear just right over the bloodstains. Even after the floors have been refinished, the stains would continue to reappear.) Though he only had use of the one arm and one leg, he kept firing his carbine rifle. At long last he was shot through the other arm and became helpless.

When the Yankees charged up to him, he uttered, "I never figured to ever surrender, but here I am helpless and about to beg for my life." One of the men just raised his gun and fired into John's heart, killing him. Then he took John's carbine rifle.

Having the gun proved terrifying for the man, so the legend goes. He was heard yelling all night, "Take John Dick Adams away from here! He's come to kill me!"

It became so bad he would see John Dick Adams in his coffee cup when he sat down for his breakfast. When he heard about John wanting his gun buried with him, he called for Grandpa Spencer, John's uncle. Spencer came and got the gun, but never buried it with the body.

It didn't matter, for the man kept seeing John Dick Adams everywhere. He even saw him in every piece of food he would try to eat, but couldn't. A year after he shot John, the man died from lack of eating.

He's Gone, He's Gone!—Richmond

Jefferson Davis, President of the Confederate States of America during the Civil War, spent the time in what is now the White House of the Confederacy in Richmond. The place is located at the southeast corner of 12th and East Clay Streets. First owned by John Brockenbrough, this home was designed by architect Robert Mills from Charleston. It was remodeled in the 1840s; in 1857, a third floor was added. Then in 1861, the city of Richmond bought it and offered it to Davis and his family. He would not accept it free of charge under those conditions, so he ended up renting it.

Varina Davis left her children playing downstairs, on April 30, 1864, while she went to make President Davis his lunch. Joe Davis,

White House of the Confederacy.

along with his older brother, Jeff, went outside to the balcony out back. Joe climbed the rail and lost his footing, falling fifteen feet to the pavement below and fracturing his skull. A nursemaid, Catherine, ran to tell the Davises. He was still alive when his parents reached him, but not long after, he expired.

And now for the legend. For thirty years after Davis moved out of the White House of the Confederacy in 1865, a little boy who looked to be five years old would be seen wandering along east Clay Street, crying and saying, "He's gone! He's gone!" Then he'd fade away.

On May 30, 1893, the body of Jefferson Davis returned to Richmond from New Orleans where it had been buried. The body lay in state at the rotunda of the Capitol for a day; then on May 31st, it was loaded onto a caisson draped in black netting. Drawn by six white horses, Jefferson Davis took his final journey to Hollywood Cemetery where he was buried for the last time. His son, Joe, was removed from his former grave and placed at his feet. Once that happened, no one ever saw the ghost of the little boy again.

Maybe if we were allowed into Hollywood at night, we might catch sight of Davis playing with his son as they once did in life.

Now That's a Really A Cold Harbor!
—Mechanicville

Though this legend has nothing to do with the Civil War, except that it supposedly took place at Cold Harbor where the bloodiest battle of the War Between the States took place, it's still a neat little story. It is said a sailor courted the lady of his dreams here. When she brushed him off, he is said to have exclaimed, "Now that really was a cold harbor!"

Historians discount this colorful legend.

Orbs in a section of woods of Cold Harbor Battlefield.

Stonewall Jackson Possessed?
—Battle of Chancellorsville

There are a couple of stories reported concerning General Stonewall Jackson. One is that crowds would hang around his headquarters, hoping to catch him at "incantations." Others did the same, but for a glimpse of him praying, as they imagined him accompanied by angelic spirits that counseled him.

Another tale. as told by Civil War author E. A. Pollard, says Jackson was considered insane when he made his march from Winchester to Romney and Bath in the terrible winter of 1861-62. One of his colonels arrived in Richmond to report that some familiar spirit had taken possession of Jackson's body; that Jackson and this invisible being would hold conversations when he went walking by himself!

Strange but true: Jackson was mortally wounded during the battle of Chancellorsville, not by the Yankees, but by his own men. It appears that at around 9 pm on a moonlit night, he and his staff had been riding back toward the Southern position. Mistaken for Yankee cavalrymen, they were fired upon. Two officers were killed and Jackson was hit by three balls. One went through his left forearm, another broke two fingers on his left hand and the last shattered the left arm near the shoulder. Later, he was taken to have his arm amputated by Dr. McGuire. When operations chaplain Tucker Lacy saw the wrapped up limb, he was afraid that souvenir hunters might try to steal it and took it to the family burial grounds of his home site at Ellwood. It seemed that Southerners thought of any kind of object linked with the wounding and death of Jackson as sacred.

There's a little myth that claims Dr. McGuire's spirit was seen carrying Jackson's amputated arm. This is hard to imagine, when it was buried at Ellwood by Lacy. But then again, maybe McGuire is trying to take the arm to Jackson, to reattach it, so that the Confederate general can be a whole man in the afterlife.

But though he survived the amputation of the arm well, suddenly Jackson took a turn for the worse. He developed pneumonia. His faith though, remained, and even at death's door, he said, "I am not afraid to die; I am willing to abide by the will of my Heavenly Father. But I do not believe I shall die at this time; I am persuaded the Almighty has yet a work for me to perform."

It didn't come to pass, for as recorded, Jackson passed away at 3:15 pm on May 10, 1863. Jackson's spirit has never been seen anywhere. It seems that he is happy with the afterlife.

There is an evil omen in connection with Jackson, though. Twenty-four years after Stonewall's death, A. L. Long, who had served as military secretary to Robert E. Lee, wrote of something that happened on the morning of the fateful shooting. He was there with Jackson at the time.

First to arise from bivouac, Jackson noticed a staff officer, General W. N. Pendleton, without covers, and spread his overcoat over him. Jackson then nestled by a small fire and Long joined him. Long got Jackson a cup of coffee as he complained of being cold. As they were talking, Jackson's sword toppled with a loud clank from the tree it had been leaning against to the ground. Long picked it up and handed it over to Jackson, who buckled it on. With a few words to General Lee, Jackson mounted his horse and rode off.

Long wrote about this because he felt it to be an evil omen, such as when a mirror or picture falls. When he heard of Jackson's bizarre wounding, it reaffirmed his own superstitious feelings about the sword falling.

One last bizarre incident. For a long, long time, many wondered who shot Jackson. Experts believe it came from Company E of the 18th North Carolina. A young lieutenant apparently gave the order to fire and he believed it was his men who fired the shots that eventually lead to the death of Stonewall Jackson. He suffered guilt over it the rest of his life.

His name was George W. Corbett. So what is strange about this? It seems that the man who allegedly shot and killed John Wilkes Booth, Lincoln's assassin, was named Boston Corbett.

Play for Me—Abingdon

Another ghostly legend of love lost at the Martha Washington Inn concerns a young woman, Beth. It is said that she returns once in a while to tend to a young man, John Stoves, who was brought in when the place was a makeshift hospital. In what is now Room 403, Beth tended to him, changing his bandages and trying to give comfort. When he found she played the violin, he begged her to play for him. Her playing seemed to bring him ease from his pain and he would fall asleep. The legend goes on to say that as he drifted closer to death's door, Beth fell in love with him.

He summoned her to his room one day and asked her to play for him one last time. As she did, he closed his eyes and died. She grabbed his hand and cried. Never getting over the shock of his death, she passed away herself a few weeks later, some said of a broken heart. An alternate, more likely truer version of the tale says she died from typhoid fever.

Since then, there are those who say they've seen an apparition with long flowing hair passing though the closed door of Room 403. And others have heard, late at night, the soft refrain of a violin playing.

Next time you come to stay at the Martha Washington Inn, request Room 403. Just don't be surprised if you are treated to a violin concert.

Jeb Stuart Rides Again — The Chickahominy River

Known as "Jeb," Stuart was probably the most famous cavalryman of the Civil War. Struck down at age thirty-one by a Union sharpshooter's bullet, his exploits during the Civil War made the stuff of legends, except they were real. His full name was James Ewell Brown Stuart.

There was the time he rode one night into Stonewall Jackson's camp, unbuckled his saber, and climbed into Jackson's bed. Jackson retorted, "General Stuart, I am always glad to see you here. You might select better hours sometimes . . . but General, you must not get into my bed with your boots and spurs on and ride me around like a cavalry horse at night!"

Stuart became mortally wounded at the Battle of Yellow Tavern near Ashland on May 11, 1864. Taken to the home of his brother-in-law, Charles Brewer, on West Grace Street in Richmond, he passed away May 12, 1864, at 7:30 pm. The next day, he was buried in Hollywood Cemetery, attended by President Jefferson Davis and hundreds of local residents.

The ghostly ride of Stuart's historic crossing of the Chickahominy, is now a reenactment of one he traveled in 1862. In 1962, two Virginia couples picnicked at the very spot. One of the men, was named Edmund Farley and the other Bill Latane—the great, great grandson of Captain William Latane who rode with Stuart during that fateful ride.

Farley had wandered away to search for clues to where the Forge Bridge may have been. Growing sleepy, he lay down to fall asleep. When he woke up, he heard noise like men building a bridge, but no one was there! He then noticed a figure dressed in a Confederate officer uniform with a yellow sash and black thigh-high boots lying on the ground, and, thinking the man was dead, touched him and found him breathing. The man had a black felt hat with a long plume tucked under its band and a beautiful sword. The man's eyes opened and he smiled. He went on to tell Farley that his men were working hard on building the bridge in time before the Yankees came. But if it were not finished in time, then they would have excitement.

Farley ambled away, wondering if he hadn't stepped into a historical time warp. More likely a reenactment was going on.

The others had their own experience. They saw a troop of Confederates on horseback, led by the same figure Farley had seen on the ground. Bill Latane noticed Union soldiers too and wondered if a reenactment was going on. He saw something white on the ground and bent over to pick it up and saw that it was a white handkerchief. Strangely enough, his initials, "W. L." were stitched into it. Just then, before his eyes, they charged, and one of them struck a federal officer in the neck and was shot, falling to the ground. As it looked too realistic to be a reenactment, Latane wondered if he had witnessed his ancestor's demise. He then noticed blood on the handkerchief he held. He looked up to see a convoy of modern military vehicles. The soldiers had vanished.

Later, Latane took his handkerchief to a museum and had it authenticated as a genuine Civil War artifact. As for Farley, he contacted authorities about a reenactment that day but was told it had been cancelled due to the military convoy.

Picture of Ulysses Grant Won't Stay Put —Nokesville

In an old house at Broadlands Farm in Nokesville, south of Manassas, the homeowners tried to keep a picture of General Ulysses S. Grant hung up. The story goes that it kept crashing down and they blamed it on some lingering spirit of a young girl. Apparently she lived in the house during the Civil War when it served as a hospital and was allegedly shot.

A curious thing, once they replaced it with a mirror that weighed twice as much as Grant's picture, the mirror never once fell off the wall.

Robert E. Lee's Psychic Prophesy —Near Fredericksburg

Did Robert E. Lee have psychic abilities or was he just a gifted military strategist? Whatever the case, after the Battle of the Wilderness, in May 1864, he rode through the field of dead bodies and indicated to General John B. Gordon his high estimate of Ulysses Grant's genius for war. He gave the order for Gordon to move to Spotsylvania Courthouse.

When Gordon posed the question whether Grant had suffered heavy losses and was preparing to retreat, Lee replied that Grant would not retreat but move to the courthouse. Lee added, "I am so sure of it that I have a short road cut to that point and you will move by that route."

The strange thing: the arrival of Grant's troops at Spotsylvania coincided with the head of the Confederate column and the beginning of the big battle at Spotsylvania.

Was Lee psychic? We'll never know.

The Lady of Luray Legend-Page County

Nestled between 211 and 340 is Luray, Virginia, famous for its caverns discovered in August 1878 by Andrew Campbell and Benton Stebbins. The Smithsonian has declared the caverns more completely and profusely decorated with stalactites and stalagmites than anywhere else. It is also the largest caverns in Virginia.

Though no great battle had been fought here during the Civil War, still there was a lot of movement through Page County. There is also a ghost story associated with the area, recorded by artist-author James Reynolds in his book, *Ghosts in American Houses*.

The story begins in the early 1800s, where a man named Pardue, with his wife and two slaves, Mammy Duro and Domeny, settled in the county and built a house in the mountain foothills bordering a forest. But he died of an enlarged spleen, leaving his wife a widow.

It wasn't long before the widow had suitors. One of them, a "ne'er-do-well" named Ham Corry, persuaded her to marry him. They had a daughter, Henrietta, but everyone called her Hetty.

Wild and independent, the girl was different from everyone else and kept mostly to herself. As the Civil War drew nearer, she grew into a free-spirited teenager who rode her favorite steed away from home many times.

During one of these wanderings, she came across an old iron pot, most likely long abandoned by trappers or loggers. She gathered lots and lots of glass jars and jugs and made wild grape jelly, sweetened with wild honey, in it. To repay those she took the jars from, she'd leave jars of her fresh jelly on their doorsteps. She saved the best for her mother though, who was in frail health. Della Corry passed away when the girl was nineteen and her father died not long after from a blow from a horseshoe to his head. Hetty had never been close to him and his death didn't affect her. She just kept making her jelly and spending the winters indoors reading.

In 1862, after Stonewall Jackson fought in the Battle of the Bank near Winchester and the threat of Yankee invasion filled the area, things took a strange turn. Hetty sent her two servants away to a farm she had bought for them on the Mary-Ann Creek. Living like a hermit now, she nailed her house tight and not a tiny bit of light shone in. She continued making her jelly. She also dressed like a man as seen by people whenever she ventured into Luray or Newmarket to sell a load of jelly and some of her chickens.

But it was when she chased a man away with her rifle that the sheriff went around to her house. Not getting an answer to his knocking, he forced his way in. Inside, he found a box of bloodstained bandages and dozens of empty bottles of liniment. It looked like she had been nursing someone severely wounded. In Hetty's bedroom, the sheriff found a ragged and bloodstained uniform of a rifleman of the Northern Army. They searched for her and came to the cabin Hetty gave to her servants. Mammy Duro had died, but Domeny was still alive. He met them at the door and admitted that "Miss Hetty" was there, dying.

She told the sheriff what happened. She found a young Union soldier in the woods near her home. She took him back to her place, hid him, and nursed him. In the meantime, she fell in love with him.

The soldier did not return her affections. Instead, he snuck up on her with a rifle while she was boiling wild grapes, intending to rob her and leave her. Defending herself, she doused him with scalding grape juice. That was the man she had been seen chasing.

She expired. Right then, the legend began.

Her ghost would be seen in the woods, tending a pot, the odor of grapes in the air. Sometimes the odor was smelled in her home. She even appeared to one couple in 1880s, her rifle in hand, and she chased them off.

Psychic Premonition
—Somewhere in Shenandoah Valley

A legend that has been passed down in the Donnely family, this story was also recorded in the book *Beyond the Limit of Our Sight* by Elizabeth Proctor Briggs, along with newspaper accounts, too.

Bridget Donnely and her husband, Gabriel Shank had known each other since the 1850s. They married one another in 1863. Shortly after, Gabriel became a Confederate soldier and went off to war. He was wounded in battle and put into a hospital in Staunton. While there, he learned that Bridget was pregnant with his baby. Afterwards, he was released and sent back to the fighting. Not long after, he was captured and taken to a Federal prison, where he contracted small pox, becoming deathly ill.

Bridget never knew this and one day, as she awaited her child's birth, she stood before the door that led to the parlor where she and her husband had married. Something compelled her to enter, so, getting the key from her mother, she unlocked the door and went in. Once inside, she closed her eyes and began to cry, unable to stop.

When she felt able to reopen her eyes, she found herself looking at the old marble-topped table that had served as the altar during her wedding. It was glowing! Approaching it, she saw a pointed taper on an exquisite saucer that she had never seen before. Lit, the taper held a tiny flame, but no wax melted or dripped down it. She couldn't understand how it came to be inside a locked room or who'd lit the candle. She also felt some unseen presence in the parlor.

She ran to get her mother and showed her the burning taper. Her mother sensed something, too—nothing ominous, more like a feeling of "smiling" that accompanied the rosy flame. Both women felt a distinctive chill as they left the parlor.

Later, Bridget returned to the parlor and found it dark, the taper and saucer both gone. Not knowing why, she said, "Goodbye, goodbye." She left the room.

Ten days later, she received word, from Virginia prisoners released from the same prison as Gabriel, that her husband had passed away from disease and neglect. This had happened on same day that the mysterious burning taper in the saucer made its appearance in the parlor.

Shocked from the news, Bridget screamed and tore at her hair. That night, she gave birth to a baby girl. Underneath the baby's dark, silky hair, on the scalp on each side, were discovered clear imprints of ten finger marks.

That baby grew up to become Mrs. Rebecca Kilpatrick, who eighty years later, demonstrated psychic abilities—the same as the circumstances that surrounded her birth. She lived with her daughter, Hannah, and Hannah's husband during the 1940s at that time. One night at about 9:30 pm, Hannah and her husband returned home to find her mother's bedroom dark. Hannah entered to check on her mother and found her distracted. Rebecca asked about Hannah's sister, Anna, who lived in Baltimore. Hannah told her she was fine. But the next day, word came by telephone that Anna had passed away the previous night. When Hannah went to tell her mother, Rebecca said that she knew and had seen her apparition, in a gray dress with ruffles at the neck and wrists, by her bed. She had a deep red American Beauty rose clutched in her right hand.

When Rebecca viewed her daughter in her coffin, she was dressed in the same dress as she had seen her that night. Her right arm lay across her body, and cupped in her hand was a deep red American Beauty rose. The examiner reported that Anna had died at 9:30 pm, the same time her apparition had appeared to her mother!

Scratching at the Walls—Hopewell

The Appomattox Manor in Hopewell is the setting for a Civil War ghost story that is not true. Built in the late 1700s, it had expansions added later on by the Eppes family. It was abandoned by the Eppeses during the Civil War, and General Ulysses Grant used it as his headquarters.

The legend tells of a nurse who hid a Union soldier in the wall of the basement when Confederate soldiers came to inspect the house. Unable to escape, he remained there even after the nurse had been taken away. Of course, he died. It is said that he can be heard scratching at the walls to be let out.

But Jimmy Blankenship, the curator for the Petersburg National Battlefield, never saw any proof for that story. He said that it sounded like something Edgar Allan Poe might have dreamed up.

Appomattox Manor at City Point, in Hopewell.

Noisy Ghost—Varina

The Varina Battlefield Cemetery has a very strange ghost that lurks around the graves. He watches over the graveyard. There's a water fountain in the yard and the rumor is, if you drink from it, this spirit will make noises and sometimes throw things at you. He is believed to be a Confederate solder.

Dark Bird of Death—Chesterfield

There is a story attached to Clover Hill, home of Judge James E. Cox, in Chesterfield County. This was the place where, before the surrender at Appomattox, General Robert E. Lee, along with General Longstreet and their staffs, were invited to a noon-day meal on April 3, 1865. After that meal, Lee mounted his horse, Traveler, and moved on to Appomattox. This was his last meal under anyone's roof until after his surrender.

There are legends that abound about this plantation home. One of these tales concerns a black bird that swoops through a window at the approach of death. Another is of a mysterious rapping at a door when an adult member of the family is to die. There are stories of banshees seen among the Lombardy trees. Mysterious deaths, dismemberment of a spring, and a tale told over and over of "Cox's Snow." The Cox Snow story is about Dr. Joseph Edwin Cox who had been to Petersburg to attend to a patient and was on the way back during the blizzard of 1857. Snow piled higher than fence posts and the wind roared wild when the doctor's horse and buggy arrived at the gates of Clover Hill. He called out, but no one in the house heard him except one slave, who thought it was someone else around the house. No one would open the door either, not even his daughter, as they were all getting ready for bed. The next morning they found his horse and buggy at the gate, with no one in it. They searched and found him not far away, frozen to death.

Another story of the black bird that is a harbinger of doom to the family happened during the early years of the Civil War. Judge Cox sat alone in the parlor and heard the sound of flapping wings. A black bird appeared, circled his head, and flew out the window. A few days later his wife and he made the trip to Norfolk; their servants said they did so because of the bird. They found their son ill and brought him back home. The day after Christmas he died.

Did Judge Cox see a portent of his son's death or just a harmless bird that had gotten indoors? The Coxes called it coincidence. The servants called it "hants." What do you believe?

The Phantom Stage—Valley Pike

There are those who say it's true, but it's the stuff of ghostly lore and legends. That's the tale of the phantom stage, and it starts during the Civil War. Beginning in New Market, a Federal spy stole a coach and used it to warn Union General Banks of Stonewall Jackson's impending attack. But two Confederate soldiers noticed it and rode off in pursuit. As they drew closer to the coach, lightning flashed across the sky and they saw him urging the horses to go faster. He turned and pulled out his pistol and he saw theirs. Just then, another brilliant flash of lightning lit the sky and the roar of thunder rolled over the coach. Another bolt of lightning streaked down from the heavens and struck the stagecoach. A burst of flames and an explosion, and the driver just vanished—destroyed.

The Confederates returned to Jackson with their story. This made the General happy, knowing that Banks would not be warned of his attack.

The war ended and time passed. But on certain nights, when lightning appears in the sky, there are stories of a spectral stagecoach rumbling along U.S. Highway 11 (once it was Valley Pike). The driver cracks the reins, urges on the fleeing horses, and then with a flash of lightning, it all vanishes.

Restless Confederate Soldiers—Henrico

At the end of Shirlydale Avenue in Henrico County, there was a house that was torn down in the 1980s. It had been a two-story building painted gray and had a basement. During the Civil War, the place had been used as a Confederate hospital. As they were clearing the property to build the apartments that stand there today, they found several graves, but no tombstones.

There are rumors that spiteful Union soldiers had come into the area, found that the house was being used as a hospital for Southern soldiers, and killed the patients in the hospital as they rested. They buried the soldiers in unmarked graves. There are tales that you can still hear the Confederate soldiers as they scream and moan. It is said that they have been seen walking up through the woods where the house was, trying to get help. Voices are heard and a harmonica playing, and sometimes the light of a campfire have been seen. When anyone goes to investigate the fire, they find that there is no fire at all.

Ghostly Encounter in Abingdon Church —Gloucester

Recorded in *Stories of Old Gloucester* by Caroline Baytop Sinclair, there is a story set during the Civil War, concerning Abingdon Church. On a dark and stormy night, in 1862, a lone Federal cavalryman returned from his station at Gloucester Point. Separated from his troop, he stumbled upon the church. Cold, tired, wet, and miserable, he and his horse sought shelter. He led his horse inside. Obviously just vacated by troops, the place was in disorder. He saw pews and paneling broken and charred wood and ashes scattered along the stone floor.

As he stood there, he sensed he was not alone. He spied movement in the north gallery thanks to the intermittent light from the lightning. Something white and tall descended the stairway. Just then, another bolt of lightning flashed and he saw a filmy human-like apparition. He could see through it!

Frightened, the soldier mounted his steed and crashed through the door and across the churchyard. But when another flash of lightning streaked across the sky and lit up the area, he looked back and saw that someone had hitched a ride with him on his horse!

Actor Scott Craig Jones performing as Edgar Allan Poe.

Chapter Thirty-Six
Quoth the Raven
—Edgar Allan Poe

"I became insane, with long intervals of horrible sanity."

~Edgar Allan Poe

Edgar Allan Poe is the father of science fiction, the mystery, the short story, and of course, he penned scary horror tales and poetry, too. There are speculations of how he died and other theories of why he acted the way he did when alive. No longer a man or just a writer, he is now an icon, a legend with many mysteries of his life and death. He was the first well-known American writer to try to earn a living through writing alone, resulting in a financially difficult life and career. Today, there are the Edgar Allan Poe Society in Baltimore, Maryland, and the Poe Museum in Richmond, Virginia. You can find out more about the Poe Museum at http://www.poemuseum.org/.

He was born as Edgar Poe in Boston, Massachusetts, where his mother, Elizabeth Arnold Poe, had been employed as an actress. Elizabeth died in Richmond on December 8, 1811, and Edgar was taken into the family of John Allan, a member of the firm of Ellis and Allan, a local tobacco-merchant, but the Allans never legally adopted him. He attended schools in England and Richmond, then started at the University of Virginia on February 14, 1826. Though he did well and passed his courses, Mr. Allan did not give him enough money for expenses. Poe made debts Mr. Allan did not approve of and refused to let him return to the University. Both men quarreled and Poe was driven from the Allan home without money.

Poe's publishing career began humbly, with an anonymous collection of poems, *Tamerlane and Other Poems,* in 1827, credited only to "a Bostonian." It is now a rare book and a single copy of it sold for $200,000.00.

On May 26, 1827, he enlisted in the Army. Two years later, when he was promoted to the rank of sergeant-major, and with Mr. Allan's aid, he received a discharge from the Army. From there, he went to Baltimore to live with his aunt, Mrs. Maria Poe Clemm, existing on the small amounts of money sent by Mr. Allan until he received an appointment to the U.S. Military Academy at West Point. At that time, he also published another book of poetry. Not long after, Poe quarreled with Mr. Allan and got dismissed from the academy. He moved to live with his aunt in Baltimore again, and some time after, married his cousin, Virginia Clemm in Richmond May 16, 1836. Poe went to work as editor for the *Southern Messenger* in Richmond until January 1837.

Not much of his life is known after that, except for the stories and poems he published, including "The Raven." Virginia became very ill and died on January 30, 1847. After her death, Poe may have yielded more often to a weakness for drink. The circumstances of his death remain a mystery. After coming back from Norfolk and Richmond, where he had done lectures, he was found in Baltimore in a pitiable condition. He was taken unconscious to a hospital and left the mortal world on Sunday, October 7, 1849. He was buried in the yard of Westminster Presbyterian Church in Baltimore, Maryland.

With such an interesting life and the mystery surrounding his death, it is no surprise that myths sprung up about him. One of these myths is the one that Baltimore claims he is theirs. Born in Boston and raised mostly in Richmond, he can be claimed more legitimately by either of these two cities than by Baltimore.

Another myth has him expelled from West Point for nudity, wearing only a belt and sword. And the story about him deserting the Army is not true. He actually hired a substitute instead—back then a man in the service could do this. He wasn't kicked out of UVA, as another story says, he just couldn't go back due to lack of money and Mr. Allan not permitting it as I mentioned earlier.

Poe made his own contributions to the myths that swirled about him. He lied about his own age and claimed he was the grandson of some man named MacDonald.

And the last myth concerns his death. He did not die drunken in a gutter, but in a hospital.

Whether the stories are truth or falsehood, Edgar Allan Poe is an interesting personality. He contributed much to literature, and became a legend after his death. Many authors and poets today try to pattern themselves after him, trying to become the next Poe. But there can be only one Poe. No one else.

Quoth the raven, "Nevermore!"

Chapter Thirty-Seven
George Washington

"A slender acquaintance with the world must convince every man that actions, not words, are the true criterion of the attachment of friends."
~George Washington

There is a myth about George Washington having wooden teeth. He did have false teeth, but not teeth made of wood. As a matter of fact, the materials used in his false teeth were probably more uncomfortable than if they had really been made of wood. Made of cow's teeth, human teeth, and elephant ivory set in a lead base with springs, his false teeth allowed him to open and close his mouth, but they fit poorly and distorted the shape of his mouth. (Just thinking about it has my own teeth hurting.)

Did George Washington ever really throw a silver dollar across the Potomac River? No, this popular myth is often told to illustrate his strength and never really happened. The Potomac River is over a mile wide. There could be no way he could have done this. Besides, there were no silver dollars when he was a young man. His step-grandson wrote that Washington threw a piece of slate across the Rappahannock River near Washington's boyhood home in Fredericksburg. That river is much narrower. Maybe this is the basis for that dollar across the Potomac River myth.

Had he ever really chopped down a cherry tree as told over and over by school children for last 200 years? No, not true at all. Parson Mason Weems, an early biographer of George Washington, invented the story. He had made up the story of a young George Washington saying to his father, "I cannot tell a lie," to point out Washington's honesty. This is, perhaps, the most enduring myth told about George Washington.

Did George Washington stop some boys from fighting in the schoolyard? Once again, another untrue tale. The story is that when

Washington's schoolmates had a dispute, they went to him to settle it, and as he never got involved in fighting, he would prevent it if he could by not allowing the other school children to fight. This myth was obviously made up to show how good a peacemaker he was and also about getting along with one another.

When he was young, did George Washington lead his schoolmates in play battle? It was said that he would rally his playmates to form into two armies that paraded, marched, and fought fake battles. Of course, he would always be the leader of one of the armies. This is another story made up to show him as a natural born leader.

A last myth about Washington concerns the old stone house in Richmond that houses the Poe Museum. It seems that years ago, when it first was being used for paid tours, the staff said it had been the location for George Washington's headquarters. Tour guides would take people through the house and tell them that "Washington slept here." The fact is, as told by Chris Semter of the Poe Museum, it was not true at all. Another myth they told about the house was that Pocahontas also stayed there, which would be impossible since she died in England long before the house had been even built.

Now for some interesting truths about him. He was the only Founding Father to free his slaves and the only president who did not live in Washington, D.C. As a farmer, he grew marijuana on his farm and promoted its growth. In the 1790s, the crop was grown mainly for its industrial value as hemp and for soil stabilization. It would be hundreds of years before the recreational and illegal use of marijuana became popular. It is also as a farmer that Washington is credited with introducing the mule to America. And last, but very strange, is the account of how, on the night of Washington's death, his friend, Dr. Thornton, attempted to revive Washington. First the doctor tried thawing him in cold water, then he lay him in blankets, and by degrees and by friction gave him warmth. This was supposed to put into activity the minute blood vessels. At the same time, it would open a passage to the lungs by the trachea, inflating them with air, producing artificial respiration, and allowing the transfer of blood into Washington from a lamb that the doctor used.

Whether myth or truth, this famous Virginian and first President of the United States is a very fascinating person to learn about.

Chapter Thirty-Eight
Thomas Jefferson

"I have recently been examining all the known superstitions of the world, and do not find in our particular superstition (Christianity) one redeeming feature. They are all alike founded on fables and mythology."

~Thomas Jefferson

Whether due to his status as the author of the Declaration of Independence or due to being a part of the pantheon of the Founding Fathers, Thomas Jefferson has become an icon that symbolizes America as well as its founders. Born in Albemarle County, Virginia, in 1743, he inherited 5,000 acres of land from his father and a position of high social standing from his mother. He read law at the College of William and Mary. Then he married the widow Martha Wayles Skelton and took her to his partially constructed home, Monticello. At age thirty-three, he drafted the Declaration of Independence. Later, in 1786, he wrote a bill establishing religious freedom. He took over for Benjamin Franklin as ambassador to France in 1784, then resigned in 1789. He also became the third President of the United States. During that term, the Louisiana Purchase occurred. After stepping down from being President, he retired to Monticello. He passed away on July 4, 1826.

Jefferson achieved distinction as, among other things, a horticulturist, statesman, architect, archaeologist, paleontologist, author, inventor, and founder of the University of Virginia. He was a legend in not only in Virginian history, but United States history as well. But, like some other famous Virginians, there are myths about him too.

One of the myths told about Jefferson is that he is the "father of American democracy." He would have been surprised, even shocked to have any association with democracy because he would have denied it. He never acknowledged himself with democracy. Rather, he would have identified with the republican form of government instead. Like the rest of the Founders, he considered democracy a bad form of government.

Another myth about him was that he was hostile to Christianity and he scissored references of miracles in his own Bible. On the contrary, he attended church regularly, was a student of Scriptures, and an active member of the Anglican Church, where he served on his local vestry. He was married in church, sent his children and a nephew to a Christian school, and gave his money to support many different congregations and Christian causes. As for taking out references to the miracles in his Bible, that too was a myth. Instead, what he made was not a Bible, but an abridgement of the Gospels for the benefit of the Indians. He used his "Philosophy of Jesus of Nazareth" as a tool to evangelize and educate the American Indians; nor is there any evidence of an expression of his skepticism. Neither did he cut all miracles from his work. Though the original manuscript no longer exists, the Table of Texts that survives includes several accounts of Christ's healings.

There is a persistent story that Thomas Jefferson personally executed someone on the White House lawn for treason. This is not true. The story originated in the movie *Swordfish* (2001), where it is mentioned by John Travolta's character, Gabriel Shear. Jefferson never personally killed anyone, nor were there any treason executions or convictions during his presidency. He did help write a "Bill to Attaint Josiah Philips and Others" in 1778. This ordered the trial and provided for the execution of the murderer and bandit Josiah Philips for treason. Josiah Philips was eventually found and convicted of robbery, not treason.

There's another persistent popular myth that claims Jefferson was a Freemason. The story may have its origins due to a ceremony that marked the laying of the cornerstone at the University of Virginia on October 6, 1817. It was customary for masons to direct many public ceremonies, such as laying cornerstones, opening bridges, and dedicating halls. Thus surrounded by Masonic pomp and circumstance, Jefferson must have seemed a part of the organization simply by association. But local Lodges 60 and 90 have never claimed Jefferson as a member, either in a regular or honorary capacity.

Another Jeffersonian link to the Freemasonry myth predates the laying of the cornerstone. In 1801, the "Jefferson Lodge" was organized in Surry, Virginia. This reflected republican exuberance after the election of 1800, and was not any proof of Jefferson's membership as a mason.

Jefferson's longstanding interest in architecture and mathematics could have made a Masonic connection as well in the public mind. Actually, not one reference to being a Freemason has ever been found in Jefferson's papers. If nothing else, his aversion to secret societies made his membership very unlikely.

Another interesting story is the term, "My name is Haines." This is used all over the country whenever someone leaves a place. Supposedly, this started with a gentleman names Haines who was traveling with Jefferson near Jefferson's home in Virginia. Haines did not know it was Jefferson he was with or what he looked like. Now, Haines was a Federalist and the Party spirit ran high in those days. An opponent of the government at that time, Haines criticized Jefferson and the government. Jefferson said nothing. When they arrived at Jefferson's home, Haines thought he should ask his fellow traveler's name.

"Jefferson," said the President.

"Thomas Jefferson?"

"Yes sir, Thomas Jefferson."

"The President Thomas Jefferson?" pressed the astonished Federalist.

"The same."

"Well, my name is Haines!" And with that, the man kicked his horse in the sides and galloped away.

Though no proof of this story has ever been found, there are many references of stories of ordinary citizens encountering Thomas Jefferson, not knowing who he was.

Another myth concerns the term, "shoes." At the United States Patent Office, paper copies of patent documents are stored in special drawers called "shoes." There are claims that Thomas Jefferson made a practice of storing early patent documents in his shoe boxes. But there is no evidence that this story is true. Historians have never found any evidence that he even had shoe boxes. Jefferson always ordered his shoes directly from shoemakers and they would either be picked up by Jefferson himself or by someone else. There is no proof that a box was ever involved.

Another story concerns a breakfast meeting between Washington and Jefferson after Jefferson returned from France. Jefferson asked why Washington agreed to a Senate.

Washington asked, "Why did you pour your coffee into the saucer before you drank it?"

"To cool it down. My throat is not made of brass."

"Even so," said Washington, "we pour our legislation into the Senatorial saucer to cool it."

The earliest report of this meeting that never happened is in *Harper's New Monthly Magazine* in 1884. It has been repeated many times, in print, since then.

Tomatoes are associated with Jefferson, too. It is said he claimed they were poisonous. There is a story that, on a visit to Lynchburg, he terrified one of the locals when he paused to snack on a tomato on the steps of the Miller-Claytor house. No proof was ever found that this happened.

Regarding Jefferson's alcove bed at Monticello, it can not be proved or disproved that he designed it to be hoisted out of the way during the day and lowered again at night. There was, however, one portion of Jefferson's bed arrangement designed to be lifted horizontally, and this was a mahogany screen which closed the bed alcove from the study. In a letter to his master builder, James Dinsmore, dated December 30, 1808, Jefferson had instructed that he wanted the folding mahogany frame to fit the alcove of his bed and to be covered with paper on sides. This was because the sash was heavy and troublesome. Jefferson went on how he wanted the new screen constructed, including, "observing first that it is to open vertically, and not horizontally as the mahogany one does." Jefferson wanted the new screen hinged to open easily, making it easy to make up the bed. If the large mahogany sash were lifted daily to make a bed, there is possibility that it could have been confused with the bed itself when mentioned later. The bed being hoisted out of sight during the day is wonderful, but with no proof, there is no way to tell if it was ever considered by Jefferson.

There's a rumor that Jefferson stayed in Bedford Springs, Pennsylvania, for about two months. It was posted in quite a few newspapers from *The New-York Columbian* in New York City to *Eastern Argus* in Portland, Maine. Jefferson never went to Bedford Springs, Pennsylvania, in 1819, though he did visit Poplar Forest during this time period. A retraction of these reports was later printed by *The Carlisle Republican* in Carlisle, Pennsylvania. This shows that the journalists for these papers did not do their jobs when they verified any of this.

Related, but not a myth about Thomas Jefferson himself, is more about the paranormal phenomena at Monticello. It is said that at Monticello, the employees have often heard Jefferson himself whistling on the grounds, as he was known to do when he was alive. There have been sightings of an apparition of a ten-year-old boy wearing a uniform and a tricorn hat peering out of a second floor window. According to a tour guide during a house tours, no one is allowed upstairs because of the fire codes, and the guide isn't sure who this spectral boy is.

Chapter Thirty-Nine
Patrick Henry

There are some myths surrounding Patrick Henry, famous for his "Give me liberty or give me death!" speech, along with being one of the United States' Founding Fathers. He became the first governor of Virginia, sworn in 1776, when Virginia had already established its independence before the rest of the Thirteen Colonies. He lived at Scotchtown at one point, haunted most likely by his first wife, Sarah Shelton, with whom he had six children. His second wife was Dorothea Dandridge, and they had eleven children. He died at Red Hill Plantation at age sixty-three on June 6, 1799.

The first myth about Henry's famous speech, given at St. John's Church in Richmond, recorded in Ray Raphael's Founding Myths: "Stories That Hide Our Patriotic Past," was actually written by William Wirt, a writer, decades later. There are claims that only a few people were there when he gave it and without minutes taken, word for word, how could Wirt ever known what Henry really said?

Like two other famous Virginians, Thomas Jefferson and George Washington, it has been said that Henry was a Freemason. Extensive research of Masonic records in Virginia and elsewhere has come up with nothing to substantiate this tale.

There is also a bit of folklore involving Patrick Henry that is told in *A Treasury of Southern Folklore*.

A young fellow wanted to get married. So did the girl. But her parents objected, as she was not of age, according to the law. If he eloped with her, he would be put in jail. The young man took his trouble to Patrick Henry.

Patrick Henry said, "You really love her, do you? How much do you love her? Do you love her better than gold? How much would you give out of pocket if you could get your sweetheart and never cast a shadow in the doorway of a jail?"

"I would give a hundred guineas," replied the young man.

Patrick Henry agreed to the price and told him what to do.

"See your ladylove and have her take a horse out of her father's stable. Have her mount it, take off, and meet you at the appointed place. You will be on foot and mount up behind her. Then ride to the nearest preacher and get married. You will get arrested, but I shall see you through it all."

The young man did what Patrick Henry told him to do and the next time he and Henry were together was in court. The Commonwealth attorney said it was so plain a case that he would just state the law and the facts. Which he did.

Then Patrick Henry stood up and admitted that the law was as the prosecutor told. "I would be better satisfied though," he said, "if the young woman would take the stand and give her own account of the elopement."

The girl took the stand. The men stared at her and the judges sat up straighter.

She said, "I told my lover to meet me at a certain spot. I got a horse from my father's stable and rode it over to where he waited for me. I took him up behind me and we rode away."

"So, did you run away with him?" asked Patrick Henry, being sly.

"No. I ran away with him."

"I see."

The crowd roared and the young man marched off with his bride.

Whatever Patrick Henry actually said his famous speech or not, is besides the point. But the myths about him are equally a part of our history, too.

Chapter Forty
President John Tyler Was Never President

Today's leaders of America have myths told about them all the time. When you take over the Oval office at the Capitol in Washington, D. C., it's hard not to collect myths. One such president came from Virginia. His name was John Tyler.

John Tyler was the tenth president of the United States, taking the position one month after the inauguration of President Harrison, who died of pneumonia on April 4, 1841. Tyler served from 1841-1845.

A defender of limited federal power and of Jeffersonian principles, Tyler vetoed most of the bills passed by Congress. His own party tried to impeach him and northern politicians denounced him for bringing Florida and Texas into the Union. At the end of his term, he settled in his plantation home, Sherwood Forest in Charles City.

He opposed the secession of the South from the Union just before the Civil War. He went to Washington, D.C. in hopes of averting the coming Civil War. It was Abraham Lincoln's inaugural address though, that changed his mind, and he went back to Virginia to urge secession. Virginia joined the seceding Confederate states in May 1861, and he was elected to serve in the Confederate Congress, but died on January 18, 1862, before he could do so. He is buried beside the tomb of President James Monroe in Hollywood Cemetery.

A myth that is bandied about regarding him is that he was never President. This could be attributed to the fact that he was the first vice president to take over for a president who died in office. The Constitution was vague about what to call such a chief executive. Do they call him president or acting president? The debate got settled and they called him "president."

But historical troublemakers can cite contemporary news stories of the time, referring him as "Acting President," or even "His Accidency," a nickname that became stuck to him.

Chapter Forty-One
Jefferson Davis

Jefferson Davis was born in Fairview, Kentucky on June 3, 1808. His first wife was Sarah Knox Taylor, daughter of General Zachary Taylor. He resigned from the Unites States Army to become a planter. Sarah died three months later. For ten years, he remained a bachelor until he met Varina Howell and married her February 26, 1845. He settled on his plantation in Mississippi. Jefferson Davis did not want to be president of the Confederate Sates, but accepted the position. He was elected for six years, not four as in the Union. He died and was buried in New Orleans, Louisiana, then reburied with Varina, his daughter, Winnie, and little Joe, his one son, at Hollywood Cemetery.

The only myth I could find about him has branded him enigmatic and incompetent, even a calculated manipulator of the symbols of liberty. The Confederate President was in fact a decent and committed leader whose mistakes concerning his single-mindedness to prove he was right, even when wrong, became magnified by the war's extraordinary demands.

Today, the White House of the Confederacy he occupied during the War Between the States is a museum in Richmond. If you plan to be in Richmond or live in the area, check out the museum's Web site at http://www.moc.org/ to find out what is going on and when they are open.

Chapter Forty-Two
Robert E. Lee

The strong, healthy boy, Robert Edward Lee, born to General Henry "Light Horse Harry" Lee III, and Ann Hill Carter Lee on January 19, 1807, was the last Lee born at Stratford Plantation to survive to maturity. Because the family lacked money to send him to Harvard, where his older brother Charles Carter Lee studied, Lee chose a military career for financial reasons. On June 30, 1831, while serving as Second Lieutenant of Engineers at Fort Monroe, he married Mary Ann Randolph Custis of Arlington. Mary was the only daughter of George Washington Parke Custis, grandson of Martha Washington and grandson, through the adopted daughter, of George Washington. The couple moved to Arlington, to the Custis house across the Potomac from the capital. The land the house stood on is now the Arlington National Cemetery.

It was in Mexico, during the Mexican-American War, that Lee learned the battlefield tactics that would serve him so well later on. In October 1859, he commanded a contingent of marines, including young Lieutenant James Ewell Brown (J.E.B.) Stuart, on a mission to Harper's Ferry, Virginia (now West Virginia), to suppress an insurrection led by abolitionist John Brown. It was on the eve of the Civil War that Francis Blair, who had succeeded Jefferson Davis as Secretary of War, offered Lee command of the Union Army. There was little doubt as to Lee's sentiments as he opposed secession and considered slavery evil. In the end, he chose friends, family, and his beloved Virginia over the appointment.

A myth about Robert E. Lee is that he was a horrible man, a rebel who owned many slaves and hated America. He never owned a single slave.

Another story about Lee, though more of a ghost story then a myth, concerns his horse, Traveller, and the last house Lee lived in and died. The place is a lovely house in Lexington, connected to the Washington and Lee University that he was given during his stint as president of the university. He built a stable next to the house, for Traveller and his other horses. The stable is now a garage, but the doors are always left open for Traveller's return. You can visit Traveller's grave, just outside the Lee Chapel where Lee and his family are buried.

The day I visited the museum, I noticed an apple and pennies scattered over the horse's grave.

Chapter Forty-Three
Stonewall Jackson

If anyone is a part of the myths of the Civil War era, it would have to be Stonewall Jackson. Stonewall Jackson was born Thomas Jonathan Jackson on January 21, 1824 in Clarksburg, Virginia, which is now in West Virginia. He went to the U.S. Military Academy, and following graduation from West Point, fought in the Mexican War until 1848. He became an instructor at Virginia Military Institute in 1851, and a year later, resigned from the Army. When the Civil War broke out in 1861, he joined the Confederate Army, becoming a colonel off the bat and a brigadier general within months after that. Jackson earned the nickname "Stonewall" at the First Battle of Bull Run when his troops stood like a "stone wall" against Union forces. Jackson died of complications of an injury caused when one of his own men accidentally shot him on May 2, 1863. He was a hypochondriac, tone deaf with music, humorless, a religious fanatic, had no sympathy for those weaker than himself, and did not read anything in the way of literature to leaven his personality. Nor did he visualize things well, like maps or terrain.

One story that is told over and over concerned Jackson's obsessive eating of lemons. It is a persistent and widespread rumor that he had eaten fifty lemons just before the Battle of Gettysburg and became so ill from eating them that he was unable to lead his troops into battle. In reality, he loved fruit of all kinds and ate any kind of fruit whenever possible because he thought he had a dyspeptic stomach.

Another myth was started by John D. Imboden who wrote that Jackson, during the Harpers Ferry episode in 1861, adjusted the timetables of the Baltimore and Ohio Railroad so that most of its engines and rolling stock passed by his command, and he ordered Imboden to capture them all. It never happened. Jackson did take a lot of B&O's rolling stock, but not with such strategies.

There is a fabrication about Jackson avoiding pepper because it made his left leg itch. Another tale relates that Jackson was so punctilious about orders that when told to march at noon he would keep his troops standing in the middle of the street of Lexington until he heard the clock chime. This is also a falsehood.

One last myth concerns what is now Martin Luther King Day. Once it had been an older state holiday, Lee-Jackson Day, honoring the birth of both generals. This started the mistaken belief that it was actually Stonewall Jackson's birthday.

Today, you can visit his house, now a museum at 8 East Washington Street in Lexington and you can visit his tomb at the Stonewall Jackson Memorial Cemetery nearby. To learn when his house museum is open for tours the Web site is http://www.stonewalljackson.org/.

Chapter Forty-Four
John Wilkes Booth
—Bowling Green

We all know about John Wilkes Booth. He is famous, or maybe we should say infamous, as the man who assassinated President Abraham Lincoln. There are also some bizarre facts and stories surrounding him. One is that his alcoholic father claimed to have experiences with apparitions. Another says that Mary Surratt, one of his co-conspirators in the assassination plot and the first woman ever executed for murder in the United States, supposedly haunts the Surratt House and Tavern near D.C. The sergeant, Boston Corbett or "Mad Hatter" as he was known, who shot Booth, was considered crazy and talked to God. There are many involved in the Booth story who died strange and mysterious deaths. The strangest story yet is the one about the Midwestern farm boy who, when placed under hypnosis, knew obscure facts about Booth he couldn't have known and said he knew him in a past life. He also said that Booth did not die on the porch steps of the Garrett farmhouse.

After committing the crime, shortly after ten in the Ford Theatre, when he entered Lincoln's box and shot him, Booth vaulted to the stage and shouted, "Sic semper tyrannis! [thus always to tyrants] The South is avenged!" Then he escaped by going backstage and down the stairs to where a saddled horse waited for him. Not until April 26, after a hysterical two-week search by the Army and Secret Service forces, was he found hiding in a barn on Garrett's farm near Bowling Green, in Caroline County, Virginia. They set the barn afire and Booth was either shot by Boston Corbett or killed himself instead of surrendering. Because it has been said that no dead body had been definitely identified, the myth—completely unsupported by evidence—that Booth escaped has persisted.

As a strange footnote to the Booth legend, there are those old-time residents of the area who say that for years afterwards, whenever it rained, bloodstains could be seen on the porch, the supposed place he was killed.

Chapter Forty-Five
Pocahontas

Pocahontas was the daughter of Wahunsunacock (also known as Chief or Emperor Powhatan), who ruled the Algonquian Indians in Werawocomoco (what is now Wicomico, Gloucester County, Virginia). She was born around 1595 to one of Powhatan's many wives and named Matoaka, though she is better known as Pocahontas, which means "Little Wanton," or a playful, frolicsome little girl.

She saw white men for the first time in May 1607, when the settlers landed at Jamestown. She seemed to like Captain John Smith. Unlike her portrayal in the Disney film and others, she was not older, but most likely around ten or eleven years old when she met Smith. The first meeting of Pocahontas and John Smith is a legendary story, romanticized (if not entirely invented) by Smith himself.

Smith led an expedition in December 1607, and was taken captive by Indians. He was brought to the official residence of Powhatan at Werawocomoco. As Smith told the tale, the great chief welcomed him and offered him a feast. Then the braves grabbed him and stretched him out on two large, flat stones. The Indians stood over him with clubs, looking ready to beat him to death. A little Indian girl ran up to him. She took his head in her arms and laid hers upon his to save him from death. This was Pocahontas. She got him to his feet and Powhatan acknowledged him as a friend. The chief adopted Smith as his son, or a subordinate chief. Actually, this mock "execution and salvation" ceremony was traditional among the Indians at that time. If the story was true, then what Pocahontas did was part of a ritual.

Statue of Pocahontas on Jamestown Island.

According to Chief Roy Crazy Horse, John Smith's tale was told seventeen years after it all happened. Time could have caused distortions in what really transpired that day. In the account Smith wrote after his winter stay with Powhatan's people, he never mentioned such an incident. In fact, the adventurer reported that he had been kept comfortable and treated in a friendly fashion as an honored guest of Powhatan and Powhatan's brothers. No where in this original manuscript is there any mention of Pocahontas saving his life by lying across his body as he was about to be killed. After he met Pocahontas again and discovered she was highly thought of by the Royalty of England, and only after she died, did he rewrite his story to include Pocahontas saving his life.

Most scholars think the "Pocahontas incident" would have been highly unlikely, especially since it was part of a longer account used as justification to wage war on Powhatan's Nation.

Another myth, mostly told in movies, though some stories too, was that she was a young woman and that there was a love between her and Smith. This is a myth. She was, as I stated, earlier, maybe ten to eleven years old, too young to think of love with a white man, or for him to think of her as anything more than a little girl.

There's another small possible myth connected with Pocahontas. Was she married to an Indian man before she married John Rolfe? There's a reference to her marrying Kocoum, a "captain" of her father's tribe. She may have—she was absent from the colony for a few years. But it is just as possible that the nickname Pocahontas ("playful" or "willful" one) was applied to another daughter of Powhatan. The source says the one who married Kocoum was "Pocahuntas...rightly called Amonate" so Amonate was either another daughter of Powhatan, or Pocahontas (real name Matoaka) had yet another name.

Throughout her short life until she died of smallpox at age twenty-two, Pocahontas proved herself important in ways that helped her people. She tried to promote peace between the Powhatans and the English colonists. In 1613, she was kidnapped by Captain Samuel Argall and held at the fort for a year as a bargaining chip in dealings with her father. In captivity, she converted to Christianity, was baptized to the name, Rebecca, and married John Rolfe at the Citie of Henricus, a union which helped bring the two groups together. She had a son, Tomas, with him.

Not long after that, Pocahontas, Rolfe and their son journeyed to England with some Indians. It was there that she encountered

Smith again (whom she obviously thought was dead as that was what she had been told when he returned to England years before), and turned her back on him, hid her face, and went off by herself. It was after their visit to England, just as John Rolfe was about to take his family home to Virginia, that Pocahontas fell ill and died. She was buried at Gravesend as recorded: "1616 March 21, Rebecca Rolfe, Wyffe of Thomas John Rolfe Gentleman, a Virginia Lady borne was buried in ye chancell. Entered by Rev. Nicholas Frankwell."

She has never been brought back home to be reburied in her native soil. And that may be the saddest story of all.

Chapter Forty-Six
Legend or Not?

Mysterious Sword—Richmond

There's a quaint tale about the oldest Masonic Hall in the United States, located in Shockoe Bottom in Richmond. It seemed just after the Civil War a meeting was held and when it was dispersed, a sword discovered. They say that the Hall still has it to this day—waiting for someone to come and claim it.

Amazing Boys—Creeds

There are two amazing young boys who were friends in Creeds near Pungo in the early 1900s who amazed scientists. When they got together, these boys accidentally made telekinetic effects. Large objects, including chairs, would move toward them. No trickery could be found. Later, when they were grown men, both ran into each other in downtown Norfolk. Trash, bottles, and cans on the sidewalk started to roll over to them. After that, they stayed away from each other most of the time.

Legend or Prophesy?

Richmond Theatre once stood on the north side of Broad Street between 12th and College. It caught fire on December 26, 1811, resulting in tragedy. There's not only a ghost story connected to it, but one of prophesy too.

A chilling tale came to light about hundred years afterwards, in an unpublished monograph written by a Mrs. Nannie Dunlop Werth, found in the archives of the Virginia Historical Society in Richmond.

The story was about Mrs. Werth's grandmother, Mrs. McRae, who happened to be at the fire that night. The story also concerned Mr. and Mrs. Patrick Gibson's young ward, Nancy Green. One day short of her sixteenth birthday on December 26, 1811, Nancy had a psychic experience. Or is it a legend?

The story on Nancy Green goes that Mrs. Gibson bade Nancy go make a purchase at some store on Broad Street. As the teenager passed 8th Street, crossing the ravine, something terrible approached her and chanted, "Nancy, Nancy, Nancy Green, you'll die before you are sixteen." She had returned back to her guardians' home, refusing to attend the theater that night to see *The Bleeding Nun*. But Mrs. Gibson made her, saying that it showed proper respect if she did so. So the girl went. By midnight that night, day after Christmas, she did indeed not reach the age of sixteen years, for she perished in the terrible fire that killed seventy-two people, including Governor George Smith.

Seven months after the fire, a young architect named Robert Mills laid the cornerstone of Monumental Church. Completed in 1814, it is now considered one of the nation's major architectural landmarks and not only the grandest, but the only remaining example of the five octagonal, domed churches that Mills designed. The building is covered in funeral details and has references to the fire. The two columns feature upside-down torches and stars and drapes that are surrounded by a flame-like carving on a pediment as symbols of mourning. There is a story told on ghost walks that there are two unknown bodies from the theater fire buried beneath the church. But when I asked the worker inside the church about this, he didn't know anything about it.

An interesting fact: This church may also be the basis for Edgar Allan Poe's "The Fall of the House of Usher," as a couple named Usher preformed at the theater. One of them even knew Poe's actress mother. As a youth Poe attended Monumental Church which was built over where the theater once stood. A bit of an ironic side note: Poe's mother died two weeks before the fire, too.

Did Bellmont House Have a Brothel? —Chester

There is a claim that a brothel had been run at Bellmont House at the turn of the twentieth century. Another story tells of a man shot to death on the premises. The son of William Sadler, who bought the place during the Great Depression, found two guns hidden over the door jamb when the house was being remodeled. One of them was a ladies' pearl-handled pistol. One of the residents of the house dismissed the brothel and murder, thinking that the murder rumors were because a teenage boy was found in the nearby woods, shot to death.

How Manassas Got Its Name—Manassas

According to legend, Manassas derived its name either from an Indian source or from Manasseh, a Jewish innkeeper at Manassas Gap. Manassas originated in 1852 at the junction of two railroads which linked Northern Virginia and Washington, D.C. with the Shenandoah Valley and Richmond. The junction's strategic importance led to the battles of First and Second Manassas—Bull Run—during the Civil War. Since 1892, Manassas was rebuilt after the Civil War. It became a city in 1975, though it remained a small town for most of the twentieth century.

Chapter Forty-Seven
A Virginian Fairy Tale

"We the Fairies, blithe and antic,
Of dimensions not gigantic,
Though the moonshine mostly keep us,
Oft in orchards frisk and peep us."

~Thomas Randolph

A fairy (also fay, fey, fae, faerie; collectively, wee folk, good folk, people of peace, fair folk, and other euphemisms) is a type of mythological being or legendary creature, a form of spirit, often described as metaphysical, supernatural, or preternatural. And it seems that Virginia has its own fairy story.

Legend of the Fairy Stones—Stuart

Many hundreds of years ago, before Chief Powhatan's reign, fairies danced and played with naiads and wood nymphs around a spring of water. An Elfin messenger arrived from a city far away, bringing news of the death of Christ. When these creatures of the forest heard the story of the crucifixion, they wept. As their tears fell upon the earth, they crystallized to form beautiful crosses. Made of Staurolite (a mixture of silica, iron, and aluminum), these fairy stones, when under great heat and pressure, crystallize at sixty- to ninety-degree angles, giving the minerals a cross-like structure.

The stones were believed by many to have superstitious power, protecting the owner against witchcraft, sickness, accidents, and disasters. It is said that President Theodore Roosevelt, President Wilson, Thomas Edison, and even Charles Lindbergh all carried one of these. These stones are shaped like a St. Andrew's cross, but those rarer "T" -shaped Roman crosses and the square Maltese ones are the most sought after.

Fairy Stone State Park is made up of 4,537 acres and was donated to the state by Junius B. Fishburn, former owner of the *Roanoke Times*, in 1933. The Civilian Conservation Corps created the park, its lake, and many of the structures still in use today. The roads, trials, picnic areas, cabins, a restaurant, bathhouse, dam, and sanitation systems are all part of the original CCC construction.

For directions to this state park, the Web site is http://www.dcr. virginia.gov/state_parks/fai.shtml.

Chapter Forty-Eight
Bizarre, True Tales of Virginia

These are stories that sound like myths or legends, but they're not. The following ones are those that many are shocked to find out are true tales. Although they are not legends, myths, or folklore; they are fascinating in their own right and add to the uniqueness that makes up Virginia.

Buried Standing Up—Richmond

One unusual tale which is true and not a myth concerns General A. P. Hill. Nowadays Bellgrade is Ruth's Chris Steakhouse. But during the Civil War, Bellgrade was used by General A. P. Hill for his headquarters while engaged in a campaign between Richmond and Petersburg, and also as a hospital for Southern soldiers. Hill died during the campaign. They tried to take his body to Hollywood Cemetery, but couldn't get it across the James River due to the damage to the bridge and the presence of Union troops. He was taken back to Bellgrade and buried in the Friend family cemetery.

Now what makes a bizarre twist to this story was what Hill requested in his last will and testament. He wanted to be buried standing up. So... they buried him standing up. When the war ended, they dug up and transferred his body to Hollywood Cemetery. A statue in his honor was created and they buried him beneath it, still standing up. Sometime later, as told to me by an administrator at Hollywood, the statue, his body, and coffin were removed to another location, at the intersection of Hermitage and Laburnum.

After the Richmond Highland Games on October 26th, my husband pulled our car into the parking lot of what looked like a school and I left

General A. P. Hill buried beneath his statue at the intersection of Hermitage and Laburnum.

him there to cross the street to take a picture of the statue. It amused me to think of him buried beneath it, still standing up at an intersection, traffic passing him by. Only in Richmond could this happen.

A Stand-Up Guy—Montgomery County

There is a story about Virginian George Hancock of Fotheringay Plantation, that when he passed away, he was put in his mountain-side tomb sitting up!

Hancock was born on June 13, 1754. He began as a foot soldier as an adult, quickly rising in rank to become Colonel of Infantry during the Revolutionary War. In 1787, he was appointed to the position of Commonwealth Attorney of Botetourt County and from there, he was elected to the Third and Fourth U.S. Congresses (1793-1797).

He made his home at Fotheringay where he owned slaves. Distrustful of his slaves, he questioned their loyalty all the time and believed they slacked off when he wasn't at home. He even took out his anger on them. His treatment of them was considered harsher than normal.

He had a daughter, Julia, who passed away in 1820. Crushed by her death, he joined her in the afterlife not long after. A double funeral service was held for the both of them. According to legend, it was said he requested that he be placed next to Julia in the family vault, which was on the hill above his plantation home. He had been put in a different position from hers, because he'd asked to be entombed sitting up on a stone chair. This way he could always keep an eye on his slaves in the fields below and make sure they didn't loaf off. For years, this frightened the slaves, knowing that their long-dead master still watched them.

In 1865, a new owner of the plantation went inside the tomb with her family to see if the stories were really true about him being entombed sitting up. They found a pile of crumbled bones and stone fragments, a skull on top. Beneath it all, they discovered bones that had to be from his legs and trunk. The position confirmed that he had been sitting down, not standing up.

The tomb can be seen the best from Route 460 during the winter time.

Ill-Fated Marriage—Arlington

In Virginia's Eastern Shore county of Northampton, the ornate Custis Tomb on the Arlington Estate offers an interesting epitaph referencing an ill-fated marriage. After a disastrous union, John Custis IV and Francis Parke Custis legally divided their estate and their lives. Local lore indicates that John wished to be buried standing up and the monument marking his grave reads: "Liv'd but Seven Years, which was the space of time."

Trapezium House—Petersburg

The Trapezium House at 15 West Bank Street in Petersburg, was built by Charles O'Hara in 1817 with no parallel walls. Legend has it that the eccentric owner built the trapezoid-shaped townhouse to ward off ghosts and evil spirits, as told to by his West Indian servant, not unlike the famous Winchester House in San Jose, California. The workmen no doubt thought him crazy for how he wanted his house built on the property he'd purchased.

Little is known about Charles O'Hara. He did leave Ireland at the age of nineteen and immigrated to the West Indies where he amassed a large fortune. History does not record the reason he came to Petersburg afterwards, nor the exact number of West Indian servants who came with him, but one of them was a woman named Jinsie Snow. It was she who is believed to have told him how to build the place.

With no right angles, even the stair steps to the upper floors are set at odd angles with the wall. One room is on the first floor and there are two rooms each on the other two floors. The interior is elongated, which could be an accident of the house's irregular shape or, more likely a deliberate plan. The windows, fireplace, and staircase are all off center; there is only one door, the front door. The oddest feature is that the cellar where the cooking was done could only be reached by a trapdoor under the stairwell. As for the ceiling, it is four feet high. Odd, indeed.

On important English and Irish holidays, O'Hara dressed up in a full British uniform and sat on the front porch—a funny thing, considering there is no indication that he ever served in the military. Yet he came to be known as "the General."

Living on the first floor, he never swept the floor or cleaned, and the house became nicknamed "Rat Castle." He also kept rats, along with parrots and monkeys, so the name was doubly appropriate. When he passed away, some people took up a collection to mark his grave, since the state got his fortune and the house. A tombstone, with a harp as a symbol of Ireland, graces his grave at Blandford Cemetery on Cockade Avenue.

Trapezium House—unfortunately, a school bus parked in front so you can't see the lower portion.

With the way he feared spirits and had his house built to keep them out, did he make sure before his death to have his coffin made the same way, I wonder? The house must be doing a good job of warding off spirits, though, for there are no tales of his spirit seen at Trapezium House.

Tombstone House—Petersburg

Located at 1736 Youngs Road in Petersburg, this house has exterior walls made from 2,000 marble tombstones of Union Soldiers killed during the Siege of Petersburg during the Civil War. Sixty thousand people were killed during the siege, which lasted ten months during 1864-65.

To save money, the city sold these tombstones from Poplar Grove Cemetery in 1933 to the builder, O. E. Young, for forty-five dollars. The ones used to build the house were made to face inward and he then plastered over the inscriptions. Young even made the walkway out of them, all facing down.

Wooden markers were placed upon the graves at Poplar Grove at first. But wood is not a very durable material and the weather destroyed

Yes, the house is made entirely of tombstones!

them over a couple of years. In 1873, the government replaced them with marble ones. The soldiers' names, states, and ranks were inscribed upon these new markers. Poplar Grove is the only cemetery in a national park where the tombstones lie flat.

I found the house, located right off I-85, and parked across the street from it to take a photograph of it. If you plan to check out this house, be forewarned, it is privately owned and I doubt you'll get a tour of the inside.

Escaping the Grave
—Gaine's Mill, Near Richmond

This story came from an anonymous soldier following fighting at Gaine's Mill in June 1862. It is so bizarre, that if it had been fiction, only Edgar Allan Poe could have written such a story.

One bullet had gone through the soldier's shoulder and another passed through his jaw and came out through his neck. Still conscious, the soldier lay there on the battlefield, surrounded by the dead, both Union and Rebel. Not long after, the Rebel line advanced and formed in front. He thought that maybe he would get help at last.

Instead, unable to speak—his tongue swollen and his mouth full of blood—he heard a couple of men speaking.

They spoke of his fine boots and his good coat, and they went to work on him to divest him of them. Struggling, the hurt soldier managed a groan.

"He's not dead yet! What will we do with him?" said the one who took his boots.

The other replied, "If he ain't dead, he soon will be, so shove him in the grave."

When the soldier tried to rise up and held out his good hand, the other uttered, "No, Simon, no, I'm damned if I bury any poor devil alive; let him have his chance; we'll leave him here."

They covered up the hole they had dug and left him there. He lay on the ground under hot sun the next day, but when evening came, a kind doctor going over the field discovered him. The doctor examined his wounds and had him sent to a hospital. Except for the loss of some teeth and a part of his jaw, he survived.

House Made of Bottles—Hillsville

Somewhere in the southern part of Virginia, there's a house made up, of all things, bottles. In 1941, pharmacist John "Doc" Hope commissioned a builder to build for his daughter a playhouse made out of bottles. Glass containers that had contained castor oil to soda pop were used in construction of this place. But unlike most children's playhouses, this one stretched from fifteen to twenty-five feet.

Nicknamed the "House of a Thousand Headaches" due to the wine bottles also used in its construction, this one has stood the test of time. It is said that unlike other homes made of bottles in the world, this one had all its bottles arranged backwards, making the inner walls green.

Lady Wonder, the Psychic Horse —Chesterfield County

Lady Wonder was well-known as the famous psychic horse of Chesterfield County in the 1920s through the 1950s. For fifty cents, Lady Wonder would answer questions on a device described as "a piano-size, scrap-metal typewriter mounted on two rusty jacks that used a double row of keys topped by sponge rubber." When the mare nudged a key with her nose, a bracket was released, and a tin card popped up bearing a letter or number. Lady Wonder predicted the outcome of ballgames and elections, advised the lovelorn, and helped baffled police detectives solve cases. She even told wives who their husbands were seeing on the sly.

A Duke University psychologist came up from Raleigh to investigate the horse's alleged powers and determined that she could spell such words as Mesopotamia and Hindustan, a feat which would make her a marvel not only among horses, but also among most American high school students, Standards of Learning or not.

My friend, author Deborah Painter, was kind enough to send me a copy of her article, "A Wonder Named Lady," which she wrote some time ago for *Horse and Horseman* magazine in June 1996. I am indebted to her for the following background on Lady Wonder.

Mr. and Mrs. C. D. Fonda were looking for a horse to buy for themselves in the mid-1920s. The couple lived on Route 1, Petersburg Pike, south of Richmond. A local breeder had some colts of mixed heritage: Thoroughbred and Texas cow pony. The Fondas fell for one of them, a black filly, and bought her.

Mrs. Fonda soon after felt there was a "special link" between her and the filly. No one ever seemed to find out why the Fondas decided to use the typewriter that Lady Wonder used for her predictions. Homemade, this device was rigged up of a set of alphabet blocks and a keyboard. The horse used short-cut phonetic spellings, but when she felt like it, would spell correctly in complete sentences.

There were the debunkers, of course, along with scientists, also. Scientists like Joseph Banks Rhine and his wife, Louisa. Though their professions were forestry and botany, they had a sideline interest in parapsychology. They had joined William McDougall's department at Duke University devoted to psychic studies. Both made many trips from 1927 to 1929 to investigate Lady Wonder. At the conclusion of their tests, they determined that the horse was indeed psychic. Because of Lady Wonder, a new name for telepathy came about: ESP, extra-sensory perception, meaning perception of information through senses other than touch, sight, smell, or hearing. In 1928, when they came back, they found Lady not doing as well, and concluded she had lost her ability.

Though her tests had been poor and a lot of her predictions did not come true, still she got some things right from the 1930s to the 1950s. She located missing people, like Danny Mason, a four-year-old boy from Massachusetts who had wandered away from his home in 1951. The police couldn't find him, and when the news of the psychic horse in Virginia reached his family, they consulted the equine through some friends in Richmond. The horse tapped out "Pittsfield Water Wheel." The detectives on the case and the Massachusetts District Attorney, Edward R. Dewing, thought that maybe she meant "Pit Fields Wilde Water." They found the child's body at the bottom of the pit.

Another such disappearance case involved Frank Edwards, author of the *Strange World* series of books on unusual phenomenon. He worked for WTTV in Bloomington, Indiana, as the news editor. A toddler named Ronnie Weitcamp had vanished from the yard of his home in Crane, Indiana. He was missing for months. The authorities had searched the woods near the town and found nothing. So Frank Edwards called a couple friends in Washington, D. C., and asked them to drive down to Chesterfield County to talk to Lady. When Mrs. Fonda heard why the men were there, she didn't charge them at all and led them right away to the mare. Lady typed out that the boy was dead and could be found in sandy soil a mile away from his home. Edwards took a chance, knowing how it would be received, and telecasted the whereabouts of the child on the television. Yes, he got ridiculed, but when the authorities found the boy exactly as told, the ridicule stopped.

The horse was a wonder. When asked, she made diagnosis of illness, later confirmed by tests and examinations done by doctors. She found lost persons and more. She made hardened skeptics into believers. It shook those who wanted secrets kept secret.

Though they could have sold Lady, even to Hollywood, the Fondas refused to. Lady Wonder passed away in 1957 at the age of thirty-three. They had her buried at a small pet cemetery at the end of Terrell Drive, a cul de sac off Michael's Road in Henrico County.

The cemetery is still there today; some of the graves are well tended and many that are not. There are even some graves beneath trees and bushes that have overgrown and others are missing their tombstones. Bottles and cans are scattered around the place and gravestones toppled over, testimony that people are sneaking in at night. I couldn't find her grave at all, so I assume it's either underneath one of those bushes or the gravestone has been lost or stolen.

Though I couldn't find her grave, Lady Wonder is still a legend that should not be lost in the annals of time.

The pet cemetery in Henrico where Lady Wonder is buried.

Conclusion

Reader, you have come to the end of your journey through the pages of this book, traveling from the shores of the Tidewater region to Central Virginia, finding your way to Southwestern Virginia then heading up to the Shenandoah Mountains and as far north as Washington, D.C. Whether you believe any of these stories, maybe some, maybe all, they are a portion of what makes Virginia unique.

Next time you're in the Old Dominion check out these places. Take a tour of the caverns or hike in the mountains, or spend a day at the beach. But beware when you do. Sasquatch or the Wampus cat may be waiting on that mountain trail. Or a witch may be waiting to cast a spell over you. And if the lights go out on that tour in the caverns, and you hear someone breathing heavily in front of you, it just might not be your guide. Especially when that person begins to scream.

Whatever the legend, myth, or even unique true stories, Virginia is like no other place on earth.

Bibliography

Books and Magazines

Bahr, Jeff, *Weird Virginia*. Sterling Publishing, New York, N.Y., 2007
Botkin, Benjamin Albert, *A Treasury of Southern Folklore*. Crown Publishers, New York, N.Y., 1949.
Briggs, Elizabeth Proctor. *Beyond the Limit of Our Sight*. Lelil Books, Flint Hill, VA., 1978.
Coleman, Loren, *Mysterious America*. Paraview Pocket Books, New York, N.Y., 2001, 2007.
Garrison, Webb, *A Treasury of Virginia Tales*. Rutledge Hill Press, Nashville, Tennessee, 1991.
Kinney, Pamela K., *Haunted Richmond*, Virginia. Schiffer Publishing, Atglen, Pennsylvania, 2007.
Kyle, Louisa Venable, *The Witch of Pungo*. Four O'Clock Farms Publishing Co., Virginia Beach, VA., 1988.
Painter, Deborah, "A Wonder Named Lady." *Horse and Horseman Magazine*, Gallant/Charger Publications Inc., Volume 24 Number 4, Capistrano Beach CA., June 1996.
Quattlebaum, Mary. *Sparks Fly High: Legend of Dancing Point*. Unknown publisher.
Scott, Beth and Norman, Michael, *Haunted America*. TOR, New York, N. Y., 1994.
Taylor, L. B., *Civil War Ghosts of Virginia*. L. B. Taylor, Williamsburg, VA. 1996.
Taylor, L. B., *The Ghosts of Charlottesville and Lynchburg*. L. B. Taylor, Williamsburg, VA. 1992.
Taylor, L. B., *The Ghosts of Fredericksburg—and Nearby Environs*. L. B. Taylor, Williamsburg, VA., 1991.
Taylor, L. B., *The Ghosts of Tidewater*. L. B. Taylor, Williamsburg, VA. 1990.
Taylor, L. B., *The Ghosts of Virginia Volume II*. L. B. Taylor, Williamsburg, VA. 1996.
Taylor, L. B., Ghosts of Virginia Volume XII. L. B. Taylor, Williamsburg, VA. 2007
Taylor, L. B., *The Ghosts of Williamsburg . . . and Nearby Environs*. L. B. Taylor, Williamsburg, VA. 1983.
Taylor, L. B., *The Ghosts of Williamsburg II*. L. B. Taylor, Williamsburg, VA. 1999.
Warmuth, Donna Akers. *Legends, Stories and Ghostly Tales of Abingdon and Washington County, Virginia*. Laurell Publishing, Boone, N.C., 2005.

Web sites

http://urbanlegendsonline.com/bridgestracks/bunnyman.html
http://www.castleofspirits.com/clifton.html
http://www.halloweenghoststories.com
http://www.naturalbridgeva.com/bridge.htm
SasquatchWatch.net
Snopes.com
Wikipedia.org

Index